How Science CHANGED THE WORLD

How Robotics Is Changing the World

Kathryn Hulick

ReferencePoint Press®

San Diego, CA

About the Author

Kathryn Hulick began her career with an adventure. She served two years in the Peace Corps in Kyrgyzstan, where she taught English and somehow lived without the Internet. When she returned to the United States, she began writing books and articles for kids. Robots and artificial intelligence are two of her favorite topics, and she has written *Careers in Robotics*, *Robotics Engineer*, and *Robotics and Medicine* for ReferencePoint Press. She also contributes regularly to *Muse* magazine and the Science News for Students website. She lives in Massachusetts with her husband, son, dog, and a Roomba robot.

© 2019 ReferencePoint Press, Inc.
Printed in the United States

For more information, contact:
ReferencePoint Press, Inc.
PO Box 27779
San Diego, CA 92198
www.ReferencePointPress.com

Picture Credits:

Cover: Betastock/Shutterstock.com
 4: Guy Erwood/Shutterstock.com (top)
 4: Olga Popova/Shutterstock.com (bottom left)
 4: NASA/JPL/USGS (bottom center)
 4: Yurchanka Siarhei/Shutterstock.com (bottom right)
 5: catawalker/Shutterstock.com (top)
 5: DenisKlimov/Shutterstock.com (bottom left)
 5: Quality Stock Arts/Shutterstock.com (bottom center)
 5: Pack-Shot/Shutterstock.com (bottom right)
 7: NASA/JPL-Caltech
11: akg-images/Newscom
15: Detlev van Ravenswaay/Science Source

19: Peter Menzel/Science Source
23: Associated Press
26: Maury Aaseng
33: BSIP/Newscom
37: Kevin Dietsch/Newscom
41: Planet Observer/UIG Universal Images Group/Newscom
44: Jonathan Pledger/Shutterstock.com
48: ndoeljindoel/Shutterstock.com
51: Life in View/Science Source
57: Associated Press
60: chombosan/Shutterstock.com
62: Andrea Danti/Shutterstock.com
65: Gene Blevins/Reuters/Newscom

LIBRARY OF CONGRESS CATALOGING-IN-PUBLICATION DATA

Name: Hulick, Kathryn, author.
Title: How Robotics Is Changing the World/by Kathryn Hulick.
Description: San Diego, CA: ReferencePoint Press, Inc., [2019] | Series: How Science Changed the World series | Includes bibliographical references and index. | Audience: Grades 9 to 12.
Identifiers: LCCN 2018003239 (print) | LCCN 2018008235 (ebook) | ISBN 9781682824184 (eBook) | ISBN 9781682824177 (hardback)
Subjects: LCSH: Robotics—Social aspects—Juvenile literature.
Classification: LCC TJ211.2 (ebook) | LCC TJ211.2 .H524 2019 (print) | DDC 303.48/3—dc23
LC record available at https://lccn.loc.gov/2018003239

CONTENTS

IMPORTANT EVENTS IN THE HISTORY OF ROBOTICS

1948
William Grey Walter builds two robotic turtles, regarded as the first autonomous robots.

1954
George Devol files a patent for the first industrial robot.

1921
Karel Capek and his brother invent the word *robot* for a science fiction play.

1966
The Stanford Research Institute develops Shakey, the first mobile robot capable of planning out its own actions.

1925 /	1955	1965	1975	1985

1942
Isaac Asimov's short story "Runaround" introduces the Three Laws of Robotics.

1950
Alan Turing imagines the Turing test for machine intelligence.

1985
Surgeons use an industrial robotic arm to perform part of a brain surgery.

1959
The Soviet space probe Luna 2 becomes the first robot to land on the moon.

ISAAC ASIMOV

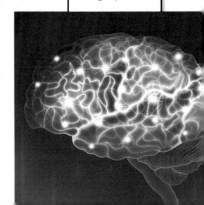

2016
Google's AlphaGo defeats human champion Lee Sedol in the strategy board game Go.

2015
South Korea's DRC-Hubo robot wins the DARPA Robotics Challenge for humanoid rescue robots.

1997
NASA lands the Pathfinder robotic spacecraft with the Sojourner rover on Mars.

2005
A car called Stanley wins the Defense Advanced Research Projects Agency (DARPA) Grand Challenge, a race for self-driving cars.

1999
The da Vinci Surgical System debuts, ushering in the age of robotic surgery.

2011
IBM's Watson defeats human *Jeopardy!* champions.

1995	2000	2005	2010	2015

1996
IBM's Deep Blue computer defeats world chess champion Gary Kasparov.

2002
The company iRobot releases the first Roomba vacuum cleaner.

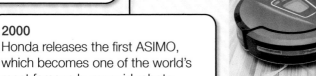

2014
Aldebaran Robotics and SoftBank Robotics release Pepper, a social robot that responds to human emotions.

2000
Honda releases the first ASIMO, which becomes one of the world's most famous humanoid robots.

Venturing Out into the Universe

Right now, 140 million miles (225 million km) away, a robot named Curiosity is driving over red-tinged rocks and rippling sand dunes. Curiosity is exploring the planet Mars. The robot navigates itself around obstacles as it takes photos, gathers samples of rocks and sand, and collects scientific data. It uses sunlight to charge its own batteries and occasionally takes selfies with a camera attached to the end of its arm. Curiosity is not the only robot to tour Mars. A rover named Sojourner landed in 1997 and was followed by Spirit and Opportunity during the 2000s. Opportunity is still running on the other side of the planet from Curiosity, which arrived in 2012.

Valiant Explorers

Robotic spacecraft have done much more than just explore Mars. They have also landed on Venus and have flown by every other planet in the solar system. The Soviet space probe Luna 2 landed on the moon and beamed back pictures in 1959, ten years before the first astronauts arrived. Robots have investigated comets, asteroids, and the outer edges of the solar system. Yet humans still have not set foot on a world other than Earth and its moon. In his book *Space Invaders*, Michael van Pelt writes, "It is a matter of fact that, until now, unmanned spacecraft have taught us far more about the Universe than human missions."[1] A human mission to Mars is in the planning stages but will not happen any time soon.

However, robotics technology has made it possible to explore distant worlds without putting people at risk. "Extreme space environments are dangerous for humans. And, robots are ideal for dangerous tasks,"[2] says Taskin Padir, an engineer at Northeastern University. His team is working on building a humanoid robot that may one day be able to set up and repair equipment during a space mission.

Robots allow people to indirectly accomplish amazing things. Their impact on human culture goes far beyond exploration and discovery. Robots perform a huge range of tasks that are too dangerous, dirty, or dull for humans. In doing so, these machines make life safer, easier, and more interesting for people.

A Robot Revolution

Experts have predicted that a robot revolution will change our lives as much as the computer or Internet revolution did. Just as it is nearly impossible to imagine life today without computers or cell phones, in the near future we may be unable to imagine life without robots. As Microsoft cofounder Bill Gates has written, "As I look at

This illustration depicts the rover Curiosity, which landed on Mars in 2012. The fourth such robot to explore the planet, the solar-powered Curiosity takes photos, gathers samples of rocks and sand, and collects other scientific data.

the trends that are now starting to converge, I can envision a future in which robotic devices will become a nearly ubiquitous part of our day-to-day lives."[3]

On factory assembly lines, robots cut, bend, solder, and weld parts of all shapes and sizes. The machines work faster and more efficiently than human workers and have allowed factories to produce more items at a lower cost. Other robots scurry around warehouses and deliver items. They have increased the speed and efficiency of product distribution. Robots help humans make more items and get those items to more places faster and easier than ever before.

Robots are changing our lives in more intimate ways as well. Robots entertain, assist, and teach people of all ages. They make surgery safer and more precise. They also help keep soldiers and emergency responders safe. Sometimes, their job is simply to make people smile. "In the 21st century robots will increasingly be living among us," says Peter Dominey of France's National Center for Scientific Research. "These robots must be able to take our perspective and co-operate with us and, if our plans change, they must be able to adjust their behavior accordingly. Most important of all, they must be safe."[4]

The possibilities for robotics technology seem endless. Science fiction writers have imagined drastic ways in which robots might change the world. In some stories, robots take over the world or enslave humans, like in the movie *The Matrix*. In other stories, like the *Star Wars* series, robots help out as friendly companions, translators, mechanics, and servants. Human characters rely heavily on these robots to get them out of trouble. Real robotics technology is not nearly advanced enough yet for people to worry about robot overlords or expect to make robot friends. However, robots are already changing life here on Earth, and they are even venturing beyond this planet. In this way, robots have the potential to change the universe.

From Fiction to Factories

A robot is a machine that can, like a living creature, perform complex tasks. It has sensors to detect the outside world, and it can act according to what it senses. Long before real robots existed, people imagined creating artificial life. In Greek mythology, the god of metalwork, Hephaestus, made tables that walked by themselves and other robotic servants. Ancient Jewish lore contains stories about animated clay statues called golems. Written instructions inside a golem's head told it what to do.

By the eighteenth century in Europe, craftsmen had begun constructing elaborate machines called automatons. Pierre Jaquet-Droz built a doll that sat at a desk and wrote out letters with a pen. Automatons may seem like robots, but they work more like clocks. They do not sense the outside world. Elaborate mechanical systems dictate the automaton's actions.

Villains or Heroes?

No one used the word *robot* to talk about machines until 1921. That is when the word first appeared in the play *R.U.R.* by Karel Capek, a Czech writer. The title stands for Rossum's Universal Robots. In the story, a man named Rossum discovers a way to construct human-like workers, only the robots end up killing their human masters. Capek and his brother invented the word *robot* based on a term from an early Slavic language, *robota*, meaning "forced labor."

For several decades, most science fiction stories portrayed robots as scary villains. But then, during the 1940s, writer Isaac Asimov popularized the idea of robots that could act as heroes. In a 1946 story titled "Evidence," a man running for mayor is accused of being a robot. An expert who tries to determine the truth says, "You just can't differentiate between a robot and the very best of humans."[5]

But Asimov's Three Laws of Robotics are his most famous contribution to the field. He introduced the laws in 1942 in a fictional story titled "Runaround":

1. A robot may not injure a human being or, through inaction, allow a human being to come to harm.
2. A robot must obey the orders given it by human beings except where such orders would conflict with the First Law.
3. A robot must protect its own existence as long as such protection does not conflict with the First or Second Laws.[6]

Asimov realized that rules such as these would be required to keep intelligent robots obedient to their human masters. But would a set of rules really work to control intelligent robots? This question remains unanswered. Robots are still too far from obtaining human-level abilities. When Asimov was writing his stories, the world's first computers were just being developed. Computer technology catapulted robotics out of science fiction and into reality.

Early Computers and Cybernetics

In 1945 engineers at the University of Pennsylvania switched on the world's first electronic computer, named ENIAC. It weighed 30 tons (27 metric tons) and took up an entire room. The *New York Times* called the computer "an amazing machine which applies electronic

The first electronic computer, ENIAC (pictured) weighed 30 tons and filled an entire room. The advent of computer technology made it possible for machines to perform calculations automatically for the first time.

speeds for the first time to mathematical tasks hitherto too difficult and cumbersome for solution."[7] The development of similar computers soon followed. Gradually, scientists and engineers improved the design of these machines, allowing them to shrink in size and increase the speed and scope of their computations.

Computer technology made it possible for machines to perform calculations automatically. They do this by following the step-by-step instructions of a computer program. But what sort of programming would allow a robot to move or perform tasks? Controlling a robot turned out to be much trickier than the arithmetic ENIAC churned through. But during the 1940s experts were already thinking about this problem. A mathematician and an engineer at the Massachusetts Institute of Technology (MIT) teamed up with a doctor at Harvard Medical School to establish a new field of science, which they called cybernetics.

The word *cybernetics* comes from a Greek word for the art of steering a ship. The science of cybernetics is about how living

The Turing Test

In 1950 Alan Turing wondered whether machines might one day think for themselves, in much the same way that a human does. He proposed a test for machine intelligence called the imitation game. It has since become known as the Turing test.

In the test, a human and a computer both have to answer a human judge's questions. The questioning takes place using typewritten questions and answers. If the judge misidentifies the computer as a person, then the computer must have intelligence. Turing assumed that it would take human-level intelligence for a machine to hold a meaningful conversation.

In the decades since Turing came up with the idea, computers have become increasingly good at conversing in human language. In 2014 the Royal Society in London held a Turing test competition. A computer program pretending to be a fourteen-year-old boy named Eugene Goostman won the competition by fooling 33 percent of the judges into thinking the program was human. According to the rules of this competition, the computer passed the test. But does that mean it can actually think for itself? Most experts think not.

creatures and machines steer themselves through the world. Norbert Wiener, the MIT mathematician, started thinking about this subject in 1940 while he was developing automatic systems for guns that could target aircraft. These systems had to be able to steer a missile toward a moving target.

Wiener and his colleagues came to realize that such steering requires a feedback loop of information. Interestingly, this loop already exists in biology. Human and animal brains use feedback from the world to direct their actions. For example, as a woman reaches to pick up an object, information travels in a loop between her brain, eyes, and hand. Her eyes and skin send information about the world they encounter, and her brain continually adjusts its instructions to the muscles in her arm and hand according to this information. A similar loop must exist in any robotic system. Engineers now refer to this type of loop as a control system or controller. A controller allows a robot to update its actions based on what is going on in the world around it.

In 1948 Wiener published a book titled *Cybernetics*. In it, he predicted that machines would become a much more integral part of society. "Society can only be understood through a study of the messages and the communication facilities which belong to it," he wrote. "In the future . . . messages between man and machines, between machines and man, and between machine and machine, are destined to play an ever-increasing part."[8]

Turtle Robots

Wiener and his colleagues studied how human and animal brains control the actions of the body and wrote about how this might impact machines. Meanwhile, over in the United Kingdom another researcher was building real robots. William Grey Walter was a medical doctor who specialized in the brain. During the 1940s he built a series of mechanical turtles that could react to the world around them. These were the world's first autonomous robots.

Walter named his first two robots Elmer and Elsie. They were small, each about the size of a toaster, and drove around on three wheels. Each had a sensor that detected light levels and a bump sensor that could tell if the robot ran into something. A clear plastic shell over the machinery made them look a bit like turtles. The machines were quite simple compared to today's robots. They could move toward light, back away from bright light, and turn away from obstacles. But these simple abilities resulted in some complex patterns of behavior, especially when Walter added lights to the robots themselves, allowing them to react to each other. Walter's work showed that simple mechanical systems can exhibit animal-like behavior.

Walter and Wiener worked across the Atlantic Ocean from each other, but they were aware of each other's work and met a few times. In 1952 Wiener noted that putting a bunch of Walter's robots into operation at the same time resulted in interesting patterns. The machines seemed to group together or scatter apart, as if they were real animals interacting. He thought that an animal expert would interpret these patterns as social behavior "if they were found encased in flesh and blood instead of brass and steel." He went on to say, "It is the beginning of a new science of mechanical behavior even though almost all of it lies in the future."[9]

The idea of mimicking life in machines has intrigued numerous researchers. Many have attempted to build mechanical minds. A field known as artificial intelligence (AI) developed alongside the related fields of cybernetics, robotics, and computer science. Alan Turing, a British mathematician, was one of the first to imagine that machines might one day gain intelligence similar to that of humans. He had these ideas during the early 1940s, before the first computer had ever been built. In 1949 he said, "I do not see why [the machine] should not enter any one of the fields normally covered by the human intellect, and eventually compete on equal terms."[10]

> "I do not see why [the machine] should not enter any one of the fields normally covered by the human intellect, and eventually compete on equal terms."[10]
>
> —British mathematician Alan Turing

Robots Get to Work

Walter's turtle robots did not perform any real work or have any immediate impact on society, and it would be a very long time before AI research affected people's daily lives. The first robots to change the world were the ones launched into outer space during the 1950s and 1960s. These included the Luna 2 probe, which landed on the moon in 1959. Throughout the space race, researchers in the United States and the Soviet Union developed the robotics and computer technology necessary to allow probes, satellites, and other spacecraft to function in outer space, away from human control. This type of robotics is called teleoperation. A human operator sends commands to the robot from a distance.

The second wave of world-changing robotics began with an industrial arm named Unimate. In the manufacturing industry, executives were looking for ways to speed up factory assembly lines. At the time, machine tools performed some tasks faster or with more precision than humans. But these tools were each only designed to do one very specific task. To change this, during the 1950s, inventor George Devol worked on developing a mechanical arm that could follow a program in order to move items from one place to another. Then, in 1956, Devol met businessman Joseph Engelberger, who realized the potential of Devol's invention. Engelberger

In the 1950s and 1960s, space probes including Luna 1 (pictured) and Luna 2 were launched to investigate the moon. Luna 2 successfully gathered information and sent signals back to Earth before crashing on the surface.

remembers saying to Devol, "You know what? That sounds like a robot to me."[11] The men created the company Unimation, Inc., to build and sell the Unimate robot. They installed the first production model at a General Motors (GM) factory in 1961. In 1966 Unimate appeared on television, delighting audiences with some tricks, including knocking a golf ball into a cup and pouring a drink.

Unimate weighed in at over 2,700 pounds (1,225 kg). Its single metal arm extended from a wide base. GM used its first Unimate robot to perform die casting, a process that involves pouring hot metal into molds to form custom parts. Unimate could also perform spot welding, a process that uses intense heat to attach metal

The Three Laws of Robotics and Beyond

Asimov's Three Laws of Robotics were intended to ensure that robots remained safe and obedient to their human masters. But in his stories, the laws did not always work out. In "Runaround," for example, a robot nicknamed Speedy travels to Mercury with two human astronauts. The astronauts send Speedy to get materials to repair their space station. But the robot runs into danger. Speedy gets stuck in a loop of indecision because it realizes that its human masters will come to harm whether it obeys or disobeys its orders. Asimov's stories reveal how difficult it might be to maintain control over very intelligent machines.

Today, many experts realize that Asimov's laws would not actually work in practice, given the ways in which robots have developed since Asimov's time. For example, many robots are built specifically to serve in warfare. These machines violate Asimov's rule that a robot not injure a human being. In addition, robots may end up needing protection from humans. As robots become more intelligent and more capable, some argue that they may eventually deserve rights of their own. Would it be fair to exploit robots as slaves?

With these ideas in mind, South Korea has proposed an ethics charter for robots that goes into a lot of detail regarding how robots should be ethically manufactured, the rights and responsibilities of robot owners and users, and the rights and responsibilities of robots—including a robot's right to exist without injury or abuse. Rules, guidelines, and other ethical considerations for robots will surely evolve throughout the twenty-first century.

parts to one another. Unimate was not the first industrial robot, but it was the first to make a lasting impact on the world.

Bringing Factories into the Future

As impressive as Unimate was, it was not easy to get manufacturing companies to believe that robotics had a future. "I had a hard time getting people in the US to take me seriously,"[12] Engelberger recalls. Most people had only heard of robots in science fiction stories. The idea just did not seem practical. But in 1969 GM rebuilt one of its plants to incorporate twenty-eight Unimate robots. This allowed the automaker to produce twice as many cars per hour and sell the cars at a lower cost. Other manufacturers began to take notice. By the 1970s Unimate and similar robots began spreading to factories around the world. Robots helped American factories compete with foreign factories by helping them make products at a lower cost.

Industrial robots sped up production because they could do many of the tedious, repetitive jobs that once belonged to human workers, and they did so with greater precision, speed, and strength. They never got tired, bored, or had to go to the bathroom. Robots also took over tasks that were dangerous for humans. For example, welding is a particularly hazardous profession. Welders face extreme heat and toxic fumes, but robots can be built to withstand these dangers.

Over the decades, researchers continued to improve the design of industrial robots. In 1969 Victor Scheinman of Stanford University designed a new robotic arm that was one of the first to be controlled electronically with a computer. It was smaller and more versatile than Unimate. Unimation bought the design and released an improved version in 1978 named the Programmable Universal Machine for Assembly, or PUMA.

"A Washing Machine on Wheels"

Industrial robots were designed to be installed in one place on an assembly line. Sensors and controllers allowed robots to move fluidly as they reached out to manipulate items. Human engineers programmed the overall task ahead of time. Once programmed, an industrial robot performed the same action over and over again and was not able to alter its plan or respond to changes in the environment. A robot that was programmed to weld two parts would keep performing its motions even if the parts were not there.

Researchers wanted to develop robots that could move around and respond more intelligently to their environments. Some worked on robots that could travel from place to place on their own using cameras and sensors. Between 1966 and 1972, researchers at the Stanford Research Institute in California developed a robot named Shakey, now considered to be the first mobile robot with AI. It navigated through a room with a flat white floor and large black obstacles such as balls and pyramids. Shakey used cameras to detect these objects and make an internal model, like a map, of what it saw. It could get from one place to another without a human driver. It did so very slowly and it wobbled, which is why its inventors called it Shakey. Peter Hart, who worked on Shakey and later founded an electronics company, said of the robot, "The ground rule was to keep it as mechanically simple as possible. . . . It [looked] like a washing machine on wheels."[13]

Academics around the world continued to construct mobile research robots, hoping that their work would lead to machines that could be used for exploration or in industrial operations. In 1977 at nearby Stanford University, a doctoral student named Hans Moravec built a robot named CART. It looked like a table driving around on bicycle wheels. Moravec went on to make many contributions to robotics, including an improved version of CART called Rover, at Carnegie Mellon University in 1983. Around the same time, researchers in France built the HILARE mobile robot during the late 1970s. These early research robots would eventually lead to the rovers that have explored Mars.

Humanoids

Mobile robots usually looked like cars or carts. But in popular science fiction stories, robots usually looked like people. Humanoid

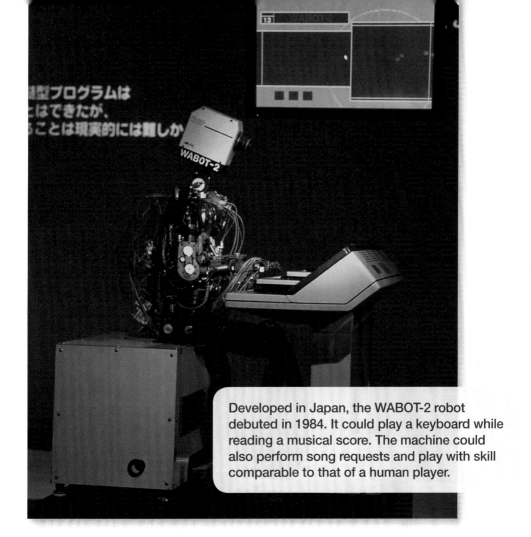

Developed in Japan, the WABOT-2 robot debuted in 1984. It could play a keyboard while reading a musical score. The machine could also perform song requests and play with skill comparable to that of a human player.

robots have a long history of attracting attention. At the 1939 World's Fair in New York, people flocked to see Elektro the Moto-Man, a 7-foot-tall (2.1 m), 260-pound (118 kg) metal machine that resembled a human. Elektro was more automaton than robot. The machine could perform twenty-six different tricks, including turning his head, walking forward, and backing up. But he was designed to do only these specific tasks, and only in response to specific spoken commands.

Most research into actual humanoid robots came out of Japan. Ichiro Kato of Waseda University launched the WABOT project in 1970. His team produced a series of robots that resembled people. WABOT-1, completed in 1973, was the first full-scale humanoid robot to walk on two legs. WABOT-2, built in 1984, was a musician that could play a keyboard while reading a musical score. This work led to the development of ever more realistic humanoids, including the famous robot ASIMO, designed by Honda and debuted in 2000.

Engelberger, who had helped bring Unimate and many other important industrial robots to market, took interest in the idea of creating human-like robots. In 2000 he said, "I want to make a robot that is in the image of the principles set out by my mentor, Isaac Asimov. The model is the human being. It doesn't have to look like a human being. It doesn't have to be physically the same, but it has to operate in our environment and use our data and our tools. And that is the challenge."[14]

> "I want to make a robot that is in the image of the principles set out by my mentor, Isaac Asimov. The model is the human being."[14]
>
> —Joseph Engelberger, the founder of Unimation, Inc.

Math Is Easy, Walking Is Hard

Human-like robots have proven extremely difficult to develop. During the 1980s Moravec observed that programming a computer to perform tasks that humans think of as difficult—such as multiplying huge numbers—is much easier than getting a robot to walk without falling over. He said, "It is comparatively easy to make computers exhibit adult-level performance on intelligence tests or playing checkers, and difficult or impossible to give them the skills of a one-year-old when it comes to perception and mobility."[15] This is now known as Moravec's paradox.

A true humanoid robot would have to be good at many different things, including perceiving the world, moving around, manipulating many different objects, and communicating. In addition, the robot must function in any environment and around all different kinds of people. That means it must be able to adapt to many different conditions. Most robots that exist today are designed to work in spaces that do not change very much. They also typically only handle one or two specific tasks. "It's easy to design a robot that can handle a specific task," says Douglas Stephen, an engineer at the Institute for Human and Machine Cognition at the University of West Florida. But, he continues, engineers have not yet managed to design "general purpose robots that can do a lot of things really well."[16]

For example, a Mars rover is great at navigating around obstacles, but it cannot use human language. A robotic assistant such as Siri or Alexa can answer spoken questions, but it cannot perform chores around the house. Meanwhile, the robots that can perform chores, such as the vacuuming robot Roomba, are unable to also wash the dishes or fold laundry. However, these specialized robots are already changing the world. Robots have spread into nearly every industry, including health care, energy, science, education, and entertainment. A future with versatile robot companions similar to BB8 and C3PO of *Star Wars* could be just around the corner.

CHAPTER 2

At Your Service

Robots and flying cars play starring roles in a stereotypical vision of the future. In science fiction stories, television shows, and movies, robots act as assistants, servants, or companions that interact fluidly with people. They often perform chores and other mundane tasks. Though it is not yet possible to make one robot that can do any job a human can, many different robots have been designed to perform a huge range of dirty, boring, and precise tasks. These robots free up humans to do more meaningful things with their time.

The most common type of robot found today works in manufacturing. More than 250,000 of these industrial robots were sold in 2015, according to a report from the International Federation of Robotics. All other robots, including everything from military and medical robots to toy robots, are grouped together and called service robots. Just over 40,000 of these were sold in 2015, according to the same report. Sales of both types of robots are growing each year, but the service robot category is growing faster.

Sorting, Storing, and Carrying

Many service robots perform menial, unskilled labor. Often, these tasks involve logistics, or moving products from place to place. These robots typically resemble small carts or cars. They handle boxes and pallets of materials in huge warehouses. They retrieve items that people order online. They also deliver bedding, food, and other items in hotels and hospitals.

The online retailer Amazon has thirty thousand robots working at its many warehouses alongside human employees. "It's certainly true that Amazon would not be able to operate at the costs they have and the costs they provide customers without this automation,"[17] says Martin Ford, the author of *Rise of the Robots*. Amazon's robots offer many advantages over human workers, including the fact that they can navigate narrower spaces. This allows the company to build warehouse shelves very close together, packing more items into every warehouse.

Logistics robots speed up every step of the process of fulfilling an order. They shorten the timeline from the moment a person places an order to the moment the order gets shipped off in a box. Thanks to robots, a person can place an order for dog

Logistics robots like the one pictured here perform menial, unskilled labor such as trundling boxes from one place to another. In the future, similar robots may be used to deliver items such as pizza and packages to people's homes.

treats, pillowcases, and olive oil one morning and then receive all three on the doorstep within two days. "Amazon bet on robotics," says Dan Kara of ABI Research, a company in New York that analyzes the technology market. "They are able to provide same-day delivery or two-day delivery because they've automated using robotics."[18]

Robots may soon make their way to people's doorsteps. One day, small mobile robots may scurry down sidewalks bearing pizza or other items, and flying drones may deliver most packages. In 2016 Amazon made its first drone delivery to a customer in the United Kingdom. In 2017 Virginia became the first US state to pass a law permitting delivery robots to operate on sidewalks.

> "Amazon bet on robotics. . . . They are able to provide same-day delivery or two-day delivery because they've automated using robotics."[18]
>
> —Dan Kara, practice director of robotics at ABI Research

Robots on the Farm

Logistics tasks are repetitive and boring, but not often messy. Keeping a farm running requires a mix of repetitive, messy, and even smelly work. Robots are perfect for these jobs. Robotic systems can plant seeds in nurseries or large fields. They can monitor fields of crops to make sure the plants stay healthy. They can apply water, fertilizers, or pesticides only when and where they are needed. Finally, they can harvest crops, sometimes without a human operator overseeing the process.

In 2017, as part of an experiment set up by a team from Harper Adams University in England, robotic farm machinery planted, tended, and harvested a crop of barley. Humans did not drive the machines and never set foot in the field. Kit Franklin, who led the project, admits that it was "the most expensive hectare [2.5 acres] of barley ever."[19] But the experiment showed how a farm of the future might run. In addition to farming, robots perform many messy, grueling tasks that pertain to construction, demolition, sewer in-

TUG Delivers

TUG is a delivery robot that works at hospitals around the world. It rolls around about as fast as a person walks, emitting quiet beeps to let people know it is coming. It finds its way by following a map of the hospital that is programmed within it. It can also detect people or other obstacles and navigate safely around them. At the Medical Center at Mission Bay, part of the University of California, San Francisco, TUG robots tote as much as 1,000 pounds (454 kg) of laundry and deliver one thousand meals every day. They can also deliver medication. To keep the drugs from falling into the wrong hands, they are locked in a special compartment. A doctor or nurse must use a fingerprint reader to open it. The Mission Bay robots also have names. "We have Apple, Grape, Banana, Orange, Pear," says Dan Henroid, the director of nutrition at the hospital. "At some point we'll get them skins so they actually look like the fruit."

Quoted in Matt Simon, "This Incredible Hospital Robot Is Saving Lives. Also, I Hate It," *Wired*, February 10, 2015. www.wired.com.

spection, and more. A world with more robots could be a world where fewer humans have to be employed in unskilled, dirty, or dangerous jobs.

Just Brain Surgery

Logistics, farming, and construction robots save people from messy, repetitive work. But medical robots play a different role— they enhance what humans are able to accomplish. In 1985 Yik San Kwoh and a team of doctors at Long Beach Memorial Medical Center in California used an industrial robot arm to drill a very tiny, precise hole into a human skull. It was the very first use of a robot to perform surgery—and it was brain surgery!

The doctors used a computer system to map the location of a tumor in the patient's brain. Then they brought in the robot, which was able to target the tumor's location more exactly than a human surgeon could. After the robot made the hole, human surgeons completed the procedure. "The robotic arm is safer, faster

Cardiac surgery with the da Vinci and similar robotic systems is less invasive than traditional surgery. It allows a surgeon to make smaller and more precise cuts, which means less chance of complications. Robotic surgery has been used for heart-related procedures such as coronary artery bypass, heart defect repair, and tumor removal. In this type of operation, the surgeon manipulates the robotic hands from a console while looking at a camera view of the heart.

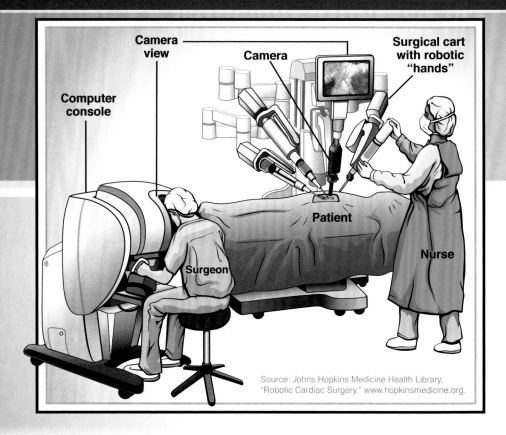

Source: Johns Hopkins Medicine Health Library, "Robotic Cardiac Surgery." www.hopkinsmedicine.org.

and far less invasive than current surgical procedures,"[20] Kwoh said after the successful operation.

Robotic surgery started to become commonplace in 2000, when the US Food and Drug Administration approved the use of the da Vinci Surgical System. Da Vinci is a teleoperated robot, meaning that it does not move on its own. A surgeon sits at a console and directs the robot's four arms using controllers similar to those used with video games. Each arm can be fitted with various surgical tools. This system is used to perform surgery on the heart, lungs, intestines, reproductive system, and other organs.

Other types of surgical robots specialize in performing hip and knee transplants, zapping cancer tumors, transplanting hair to reverse baldness, and more. Many robotic surgery systems allow a human surgeon to see the inside of the body in great detail. These systems also improve dexterity, steadiness, and comfort. Many users believe that this makes surgery safer for the patient. Dr. Vipul Patel of Florida Hospital near Orlando says, "From Day 1, when I sat down at that robotic console, I knew we would give patients a better outcome. I have not seen anyone who has done a good amount of robotic surgery go back [to traditional methods]."[21]

Amazing Medical Robots

Robots used for surgery are becoming smaller and more precise. In 2016 Dr. Robert MacLaren of Oxford University in England performed the world's first robotic eye surgery. He used a Robotic Retinal Dissection Device (R2D2). MacLaren said that systems like the R2D2 "will open the door to new operations for which the human hand does not have the necessary control and precision."[22] This means that formerly incurable eye conditions, including some forms of blindness, may become curable.

Surgical robots are making it possible to treat more diseases and are making treatments safer and more comfortable for doctors and their patients. Other medical robots play less glamorous roles, but they also help the medical system run more smoothly and safely. Pharmacy robots act like drug vending machines to automatically dispense or mix doses of medications for patients. Cleaning robots use powerful ultraviolet light to disinfect hospital rooms. Mobile robots help carry items around hospitals. Robotic lifts and wheelchairs help move patients who require assistance.

Telepresence

Another variety of robot that is showing up in doctor's offices, hospitals, and beyond acts as a stand-in for a person. A telepresence robot is essentially a virtual body that allows someone to be in a distant place without going anywhere. Currently, most of these robots look like a touch screen attached to a skinny pole mounted on a set of wheels. The touch screen hosts a video call, but instead of just talking and listening, the person on the other end of the call can also move the robot and the screen in order to look around.

Some doctors use telepresence robots to check on patients, and some patients use telepresence to experience the world. One very sick child named Max Lasko could not be around other kids because catching a cold or flu would be life threatening. So he used a robot to attend school. His mother says, "We wanted him to be able to interact with his peers but we wanted to do so safely."[23]

Robots at Home

Logistics, farming, and medical robots tend to work in professional environments. The people who use them usually undergo special training to learn how to operate and maintain the robots. But other service robots become part of ordinary peoples' daily lives. These household robots include ones that perform chores. There are robots that can mow a lawn, control a house's temperature, and vacuum or mop floors.

Perhaps the most well-known household robot on the market today is the Roomba, a robot vacuum cleaner. Introduced by the company iRobot in 2002, it was not the first robotic vacuum, but it quickly became the most popular. By 2005 over a million Roombas had been sold. Colin Angle, one of iRobot's cofounders, had previously built expensive, complicated research robots. But it frustrated him that he did not yet have a robot at home that could do chores. "I had built the robot of my dreams, but I was not satisfied," he recalls. "The visions portrayed in science fiction novels had not yet been achieved. I wanted a robot that could clean my house."[24] He set out to build a robot that would make a difference in people's lives, and he did.

Milking Cows

At a family farm in Michigan, robots will soon be the only ones milking the cows. A new system of twenty-four robotic milking stations will cut humans out of the process entirely. The cows are free to come and be milked when they want. They quickly learn to follow a milking routine because they also get fed at the milking station. A robotic attachment uses cameras and sensors to scan the cow's underside and attach a suction cup to the cow's teats. The system can even tell if a cow is developing an infection on its udder. According to Bryant Trierweiler, one of the farm's owners, "For the last few years, my family has been discussing the farm's next steps. Ultimately, the conversations kept coming back to robotics as we felt it was the best fit." The family thought that the automatic milking system would save money in the long run and also be more comfortable for the cows.

Quoted in Andrew Amelinckx, "Rise of the (Cow Milking) Robots," *Modern Farmer*, December 12, 2016. https://modern farmer.com.

A Roomba is not particularly intelligent. The first generation of the robot cleaned a room by following a random spiraling pattern, and it changed direction when it bumped into something. It also used sensors to detect very dirty areas and to avoid falling down stairs, and it could find and return to its charging station when it finished cleaning. Later generations added the ability to map a room, but the success of the early Roomba showed that robots can perform a useful function without being particularly complex.

Furbies to Fingerlings

The Roomba is a tool intended to clean the house. Other household robots are designed to entertain humans or socialize with them. On toy store shelves, robots can be found in the forms of everything from dogs and dinosaurs to abstract shapes such as spheres and cubes. In 1998 the cuddly Furby robot became a sensation. The toy could learn English commands and communicate with nearby

Furbies. In 1999 Sony released the first Aibo, a robotic dog that cost $2,000. The company announced in late 2017 that it would soon release an updated version that "can form an emotional bond with members of the household while providing them with love, affection, and the joy of nurturing and raising a companion."[25] The new Aibo uses cutting-edge artificial intelligence techniques and online data to learn from both its own experiences and those of other Aibo dogs.

> "Robots are cool. Kids have curious minds and are easily drawn to toys that bring their imagination to life."[26]
>
> —Ladislas de Toldi, the chief executive officer of Leka

The Fingerling, the hottest toy of the 2017 Christmas season, is a monkey, unicorn, or sloth small enough to grip a child's finger. It costs around fifteen dollars but comes packed with sensors and basic artificial intelligence that allow it to react to gestures and sounds. It can babble, kiss, snore, and fart. "Robots are cool," says Ladislas de Toldi, the chief executive officer of Leka, a company that makes a toy robot also named Leka. "Kids have curious minds and are easily drawn to toys that bring their imagination to life. . . . We're nearing a point where [robots] really aren't just toys anymore, but companions."[26]

More than Fun and Games

A farting monkey toy may be cool, but it does not change the world all that much. There are other robotic toys, however, that help kids explore engineering and computer science. LEGO Mindstorms kits, for example, allow kids and teens to build their own working robots. Likewise, a pair of programmable robots named Dash and Dot help teach kids ages six and up the basics of computer coding. Several different educational groups organize regular competitions that challenge kids in elementary school through high school to use these toys and others to solve engineering problems. Examples include the Wonder League Robotics Competition, the FIRST Robotics Competition, the FIRST LEGO League competition, and the VEX Robotics Competition. Students who participate in these contests gain valuable experience building and working with robots and computer technology.

Other educational robots, including Leka, are poised to have a different sort of impact. Leka can help people with autism or other disabilities learn to communicate. The spherical robot can play music, chirp, and vibrate. It displays facial expressions and uses games to help kids learn how to react to social cues. People with autism spectrum disorders tend to interact more easily with technology, including robots, than they do with people. "Many autistic people are drawn to technology, particularly the predictability it provides, which means it can be a very useful means of engaging children, and adults too,"[27] says Carol Povey, the director of the National Autistic Society's Centre for Autism in the United Kingdom. When interacting with a robot, a child with autism may be more likely to focus on the lesson and absorb the material being taught.

Leka is joined by CosmoBot, Buddy, Kaspar, Milo, and other robots designed to provide therapy for kids and adults with a range of disorders. Carole Samango-Sprouse, a doctor who has used CosmoBot as a therapy tool, says the robot has worked wonders for her patients. One such patient is Kevin Fitzgerald, who has a disorder that makes speaking extremely difficult. She says, "[CosmoBot] gives Kevin planning capacity; he gives him independence because he can select with CosmoBot what he wants to do."[28] Kids work harder and longer when they interact with the robot, she says, because the robot makes difficult tasks more fun and engaging.

Companion Robots

Providing therapy for people is just one of many roles that a high-end, interactive companion robot can play. This type of service robot is like a smartphone or tablet. It comes with some basic features but can be programmed and customized to fit a user's preferences. The French company Aldebaran Robotics has developed two companion robots: Pepper and Nao. Pepper is larger—about the height of a young child—and rolls around on wheels. Nao is the size of a doll and walks on two legs. Both have cartoony features and the ability to communicate with people. They both have a basic ability to express and detect human emotions—and both cost thousands of dollars.

Nao is mainly used in educational and health care settings. The robot can help teach kids programming, work with people with autism, and entertain the residents of nursing homes. Pepper is often used as a guide or customer service attendant, working in retail stores and hospitals, at conventions, and on cruise ships. The robot gives people directions and other useful information. It can understand and respond to human speech in several languages, including English, Italian, French, and Japanese. It also uses a touch screen on its chest to display information.

Nao's and Pepper's conversational abilities are similar to those of an entirely digital assistant such as Siri, which comes with the iPhone, or Alexa, which comes with the Amazon Echo. These assistants can answer questions about the weather, play music, look up information online, and more. Yet robots like Nao and Pepper also add mobility and a range of expressive emotions to the experience.

A company called ZoraBots wrote software that can be used with either the Nao or Pepper robot to make it a lively, interactive companion. At one nursing home in the Netherlands, a Nao robot running Zora software can be found interacting with residents. For example, the robot leads senior citizens through their physical therapy exercises. Nao and Pepper are also both commonly found in laboratories where researchers are working on new programs that will allow robots to interact more fluidly with people. The robots offer a perfect platform to test new software without having to build an entire robot from scratch.

Some people in Japan, where the Pepper robot was first released, have purchased one to keep at home. Kuri is another home robot that is less expensive than Pepper or Nao. Kuri has no arms, and its face is a sphere with two big dot-shaped eyes, making it much less human-like in appearance. But Kuri

The companion robot Nao can detect and express human emotions, enabling it to communicate with people. Here, a Nao robot leads a group of retirement home residents in a series of exercises.

can roll around, swivel its head, and blink its eyes. Kuri can also take photos, record videos, answer questions, and keep people company.

Robot Caretakers

Robots such as Nao, Pepper, and Kuri are the closest humans have come to developing robot companions that attend to people's needs. Many experts hope that these robots will become more capable assistants, especially for the elderly. This could help solve a growing social problem. In the United States and Japan, the population of elderly people is growing so fast that there are not enough younger people to care for them. "It's a crisis here," says Lynette Whiteman of Caregiver Volunteers in New Jersey. "Wherever you drive you see lawn signs with jobs for aides. There are waiting lists to get an aide."[29]

Robots can already assist the elderly with a limited range of tasks. Robear is a large robot used in some hospitals in Japan to move patients who are unable to get out of bed on their own. Likewise, telepresence robots can allow an elderly person access to nurses and doctors from home. And home robots like Nao and Pepper can provide companionship and answer questions. Aldebaran Robotics, the company that created Nao and Pepper, is now working on a robot named Romeo. This robot is intended to be a companion for the elderly. It will be able to help around the house with tasks such as fetching items, opening jars, and opening doors.

> "In the future, we might have a robot for each person, helping older people get three or four more years of autonomous living before they even have to go into a care home."[30]
>
> —Bruno Maisonnier, the founder of Aldebaran Robotics

Bruno Maisonnier, the founder of Aldebaran Robotics, says that he became determined to make better elder care robots after an older woman once stopped him in the street after seeing him discuss his company's robots in a news report. "I am disabled, depending on someone," she said to him. "You cannot imagine how painful it is not being able to decide on my own life." She hoped he would create a robot to help people like her. Maisonnier believes that robots will help give older people and those with disabilities more control over their lives. He says, "In the future, we might have a robot for each person, helping older people get three or four more years of autonomous living before they even have to go into a care home."[30]

Robots could restore dignity and independence to a rapidly growing population of elderly people. And service robots of all kinds could free people of all ages from boring, tedious, or messy work.

CHAPTER 3

Disasters, Wars, and Exploration

A robot drives a vehicle down a dirt road. It stops, gets out of the vehicle slowly and carefully, then kneels down and rolls along on wheels located in its legs. It gets to a building and opens a door. Once inside, it discovers that communication with its human operators has become more difficult. Despite this, it turns a valve on a pipe, drills a hole in a wall, then moves a plug in the wall from one socket to another. Finally, it pushes through a pile of fallen objects and climbs up some stairs. Nearby, a bunch of humans cheer loudly. This is the final round of the 2015 DARPA Robotics Challenge, and the robot's name is DRC-Hubo. Its designers, Team KAIST of South Korea, took home a $2 million grand prize after navigating their robot successfully through all of the tasks in the competition in the fastest time.

DARPA, short for the Defense Advanced Research Projects Agency, organized the competition with the goal of developing a robot that could respond to assist people after a disaster, such as an earthquake, hurricane, or terrorist attack. However, even the winners of the DARPA challenge are not quite ready to handle a real disaster. Almost all of the robots in the competition fell over at some point during the trials, and only one—an ape-like robot named RoboSimian—could get back up without its handlers coming to the rescue. The most difficult part of the competition for the robots was very easy for most people—getting out of a car. While trying to do this, one robot fell and hit its head so hard that hydraulic fluid sprayed out. It looked like the robot was bleeding green goo. In addition to not being able to get some of the tasks right, these were extremely expensive machines under the control of expert handlers. In a real disaster, robot responders would have to be cheap enough to deploy in meaningful numbers and simple enough for local teams to learn to use.

The robots in the DARPA challenge may seem clumsy and awkward compared to the average human. But it was still amazing that each robot was able to accomplish so many different kinds of tasks. The breadth of a single robot's abilities will continue to expand in the future. In 2017 Honda unveiled a humanoid disaster-response robot named E2-DR. The robot is designed to do everything in the DARPA challenge and more, including climbing ladders and squeezing through tight spaces.

Even a robot that can only perform a few basic tasks can assist in a disaster or other dangerous situation. In a war zone, in outer space, or the in deep sea, robots offer many advantages over humans. They can be made to withstand gunfire, extreme heat, severe cold, high pressure, or toxic fumes. They do not need to breathe, eat, sleep, or go to the bathroom. They cannot feel afraid or lonely. They are also expendable. The death or injury of a human being is a horrible tragedy, but a lost or broken robot can be replaced or repaired.

Robots to the Rescue

Robots have already made a difference in the aftermath of several horrible disasters. After the terrorist attack on the World Trade Center in New York City on September 11, 2001, dozens of robots probed the wreckage. Several were PackBots, a robot produced by iRobot, maker of the Roomba vacuum cleaner. This was the very first documented use of robots to respond to a disaster. Howie Choset, a roboticist at Carnegie Mellon University,

described the robots as "really cool remote-controlled cars that provide video and other sensory feedback to the user."[31]

Human controllers remotely drove the robots into tight spaces to search for trapped people and check which areas might be safe for rescuers to enter. Robin Murphy, director

Equipped with cameras, sensors, and an arm that can lift things, the Packbot (pictured) is a remote-controlled robot that is used to explore places that are impossible or dangerous for humans to enter. Originally developed for military use, PackBots have also been employed to aid rescue and cleanup efforts after disasters.

of the Center for Robot-Assisted Search and Rescue, was there at the scene. She described the spaces that the robots searched: "You can't fit a person or a dog—and it's on fire."[32] The robots did not directly rescue any survivors from this horrible tragedy. But they did prevent emergency workers from going into situations and structures that were very dangerous.

Ten years later, robots responded to the Fukushima Daiichi nuclear power plant disaster. In 2011 a tsunami caused a partial meltdown at the plant, releasing dangerous radioactive materials

A Robot Swarm

Most exploration robots are huge, heavy, and expensive. But bigger is not always better. In 1989 the famous roboticist Rodney Brooks wrote a paper titled *Fast, Cheap and Out of Control: A Robot Invasion of the Solar System.* His idea was that robot exploration might work better with hundreds or even millions of very tiny, simple robots rather than one large beast of a machine. Losing one or even many tiny robots would not mean the end of a mission. The rest of the robot swarm could continue to work and explore. Brooks and his team had already built a small insect-like robot named Genghis that pursued any moving infrared light. "When it was switched on, it came to life! It had a wasplike personality: mindless determination," Brooks explains.

Although robotic insect swarms have yet to be deployed on other planets, many researchers are still interested in the idea of robots that work together like ants or bees to perform complex tasks. In 2014 a team at SRI International (formerly the Stanford Research Institute) introduced its MicroFactory, which is inhabited by magnetic robots that are each only slightly larger than a grain of salt. Like an ant colony or beehive, these robots work together to build objects.

Rodney Brooks, *Flesh and Machines: How Robots Will Change Us.* New York: Pantheon, 2002, p. 46.

and forcing one hundred thousand people out of their homes. Toxic nuclear waste at the damaged plant made it too dangerous for humans to enter. PackBots were on the scene again, along with a larger iRobot product called Warrior. A Japanese robot called Quince also helped out. Humans operated multiple copies of each robot from afar, using cameras and other sensors to assess the situation and begin cleanup activities. Workers even taped a vacuum hose onto a Warrior in order to suck up radioactive dust.

Bombs Away

Both PackBot and Warrior robots were originally developed to make warfare safer for human troops on the ground. PackBot has been around since 1998. The current model is small, wide, and flat. It folds up to the size of a very thick coffee-table book, allowing operators to carry it around like a backpack. On the ground, its treads and a set of two flipper-like feet allow it to climb over obstacles. It can also extend its one arm up and out to grab things. The robot can be equipped with sensors to smell specific chemicals, much like a trained bomb-sniffing dog. A human operator controls PackBot using a computer. If the robot goes too far out of range and loses contact with its operator, it knows to backtrack to a place where it can get a signal. It can also flip itself over if it falls on its back.

The US Army uses PackBot robots to check areas for bombs, chemical weapons, or enemies before sending in human troops. Colonel Bruce Jette used the robots in combat when he served in Afghanistan during the early 2000s. He points out that losing a robot is a whole lot easier than losing a soldier. Writing a letter to a deceased soldier's parents is a heartbreaking task. In contrast, he says, "I don't have any problem writing to iRobot, saying 'I'm sorry your robot died, can we get another?'"[33]

The Warrior robot looks a lot like PackBot, only larger. It is almost six times heavier. Warrior can push cars around, pick up and move heavy rubble, and smash through windows. It is especially useful for checking out cars that may be armed with explosive devices. In 2011 iRobot came out with a third military robot called FirstLook. This one is tiny—it only weighs about 6 pounds (2.7 kg)—but has the same basic design as its cousins. The big difference is that FirstLook is meant to be tossed through windows and over walls. Then it can check out whether an area is safe. The hardy machine can survive drops up to 15 feet (4.6 m) onto concrete or under water.

What all military robots have in common is that they can go into potentially dangerous situations ahead of human beings. This

> "I don't have any problem writing to iRobot, saying 'I'm sorry your robot died, can we get another?'"[33]
>
> —US Army colonel Bruce Jette

helps save soldiers' lives. Major General Walter L. Davis of the US Army says that robots are allowing "soldier[s] to be more effective, efficient and protected while supporting the Army's mission."[34] Bomb-defusing robots and other unmanned robotic vehicles are also widely used in law enforcement in the United States and elsewhere. They help the police handle explosives and other dangerous situations.

Seek and Destroy

In war, not all robots are the friendly, investigative type. Others have the potential to cause great destruction. Robotics first began transforming military operations during the Cold War between the United States and the former Soviet Union in the late 1950s. It was during this time that engineers developed the very first intercontinental ballistic missiles (ICBMs). Each missile is essentially a complex robotics system that can strike anywhere on the planet by sending a rocket carrying a bomb into outer space and then guiding it back down to Earth.

What made these robotic weapons especially dangerous, though, was the fact that they could be armed with atomic bombs. The first nuclear weapons had just been developed and detonated at the end of World War II. Now, ICBMs allowed them to be sent anywhere on the planet. This meant that any country with the right technology could destroy any other country within hours. This completely changed how warfare worked. War between countries armed with nuclear weapons becomes a frightful standoff. So far, no nation has dared use nuclear weapons first for fear that another might retaliate.

Robotic spacecraft have also dramatically changed the way warfare and intelligence are conducted. Satellites are a type of robotic spacecraft that remain in orbit around Earth. Many of these satellites allow countries to spy on each other. Some satellites perform continuous monitoring and sound an alarm when a threat is detected. Others are used to seek specific information. For example, US satellites monitor the country of North Korea,

A type of robotic spacecraft, satellites remain in orbit around Earth and in some cases are used by countries to spy on one another. This satellite image shows the Korean Peninsula; the bright area in the center is Seoul, South Korea, and its environs.

which has threatened to launch nuclear weapons against its enemies. The satellite imagery helps experts assess whether the country is preparing for an attack.

Eyes in the Sky

There is a limit to how much a satellite can see from space. Therefore, militaries around the world also rely heavily on unmanned aerial vehicles (UAVs), commonly called drones. A drone is a type of robot that typically takes the form of a miniature helicopter or

The Robots of the Space Station

On board the International Space Station (ISS), human astronauts perform important scientific research. Since 2012 they have had help from a humanoid robot. Robonaut 2, nicknamed R2, takes measurements and performs other repetitive maintenance tasks in the space station. Eventually, the robot should be able to venture out on space walks to make repairs. NASA is also programming the robot to respond to medical emergencies. If an astronaut needs emergency care, a doctor or surgeon on Earth will be able to control Robonaut's arms via remote control to perform a medical procedure.

Robonaut is not the only robot on the ISS. A tiny spherical robot named Int-Ball, designed by the Japan Aerospace Exploration Agency, arrived in 2017. It moves around by itself, taking photos and videos. In 2018 NASA will send up its own monitoring robot, called Astrobee. In addition to taking pictures, this small cube-shaped robot has a robotic arm that it can extend to perform tasks.

small airplane. But no pilot rides inside. A person flies the craft from the ground, operating it as if he or she were playing a video game. Drones can take photos and record videos and transmit this information in real time to anywhere in the world. They can also intercept communications, snooping on radio transmissions. Some drones are outfitted with stealth technology that allows them to sneak past enemy detection systems. UAVs helped track the location of Osama bin Laden, the man whose terrorist organization had carried out the September 11, 2001, terrorist attacks. In 2011 a US Navy sea, air, and land (SEAL) team raided a secret compound and killed Bin Laden. During the raid, drones transmitted video in real time to President Barack Obama and other top officials.

Drones can also be equipped with weapons. Doing so creates a flying robot that can seek and destroy a very specific target. The US military uses drones to kill terrorist leaders in operations that are known as drone strikes. These operations, however, are highly controversial. One big problem is that civilians sometimes die in drone strikes along with the targeted terrorist group. But supporters of drones argue that fewer civilians die in this type of strike than in normal warfare. They say that drones make warfare against scattered terrorist organizations easier and safer overall.

Saving Lives

Drones may have started out as spying and killing machines, but they can also save lives and speed up recovery efforts after a disaster. After Hurricane Katrina struck New Orleans in 2005 and killed 1,833 people, drones flew around the flooded area to inspect buildings that had been damaged. Since then, drones have been deployed during and after hundreds of disasters. Most of these inspect property and equipment. Others fly over and even into hurricanes and other storms, allowing weather experts to track the storms and determine where they will go and how strong they will become. "This important work is making it possible to learn more about severe weather without risking a life in uncertain environments,"[35] says Steven Bilby, the president of Cherokee Nation Technologies, a company that has worked with NASA and the National Oceanic and Atmospheric Administration to track storms.

Some drones have saved lives. These flying robots can quickly locate lost, stranded, or injured people. In a typical search-and-rescue effort, a hundred people fan out, walking around to cover a large area. "Now, you can put a drone up in the air with a thermal imaging camera and be able to pick that [missing] person out very, very quickly,"[36] says Matt Sloane, the chief executive officer of SkyFire, a company that trains police and fire departments to use drones. In 2017 an eighty-four-year-old man did not return home from a hunting trip. The police sent out a drone with infrared sensors to look for body heat. After about an hour, the drone found him. "He actually was down on the ground in the wet, swampy area. So he was partially submerged,"[37] said Dave Thomson of the Rochester Police Department in Minnesota. The police believed that they would not have saved the man without the flying robot's help.

Drones can also deliver lifesaving supplies. They have been used to deliver medical supplies in Papua New Guinea, Rwanda, and other remote locations. Drones also help protect animals. In Africa, drones are beginning to keep watch over herds of elephants and rhinoceroses, looking for signs of criminals called poachers who hunt protected animals. "We want a drone to help us see things we can't see standing by the jeep,"[38] says Colby Loucks, the leader of the Wildlife Crime Technology Project at the World Wildlife Fund.

While PackBots crawl across the ground and drones gaze down from the sky, a third category of rescue robot operates in the water. Underwater robotic vehicles typically resemble small submarines. A human operator remotely drives the robot through the water, gathering video and other data. SARbot is a small shoebox-sized underwater robot that was originally designed to salvage shipwrecks. However, it has also been used to assess damage after disasters. In addition, some emergency-response teams plan to use the robot to assist people who are drown-

Drones, unmanned flying robots that resemble a small aircraft and are operated remotely, are used for numerous purposes. In Africa, officials use them to search for poachers who hunt protected animals including elephants and these rhinoceroses.

ing. "The next time you hear about a disaster, look for the robots," says Robin Murphy, who continues to lead robotic rescue efforts. "They may be underground, they may be underwater, they may be in the sky, but they should be there."[39]

Deep Sea and Outer Space Explorers

Rolling, walking, flying, and diving robots extend the reach of human soldiers, police officers, and emergency responders. They allow people to scout out areas that are either too difficult or too dangerous to approach. Sometimes, though, the remote locations that robots visit have nothing to do with wars or disasters. These exploration robots investigate the deep ocean and outer space in pursuit of scientific discoveries.

In 2009 the robot Nereus descended down into the Mariana Trench in the Pacific Ocean, the deepest place on Earth. It was not the first time a machine had reached this depth, but Nereus was the first that could continue to take pictures and collect samples in such deep places. Unfortunately, Nereus was destroyed in 2014 during one of its dives in what seemed to be an implosion. But other deep sea robotic explorers are still hard at work inspecting boat bottoms, identifying submerged debris, and performing surveys or gathering samples for scientific research.

> "The next time you hear about a disaster, look for the robots. They may be underground, they may be underwater, they may be in the sky, but they should be there."[39]
>
> —Robin Murphy, the director of the Center for Robot-Assisted Search and Rescue

Most undersea robots resemble boxes or scuba diving tanks. But one—known as OceanOne—is a humanoid. OceanOne acts as a remotely operated robot diver. While the robot is diving under the water, a human operator watches what the robot sees on a computer screen. Joystick controllers allow the operator to reach out and grab objects. The operator can even feel what the robot feels through a touch feedback system in the joysticks.

In 2016 Oussama Khatib, a computer scientist at Stanford University who designed OceanOne, piloted the robot down to recover treasures from a seventeenth-century shipwreck. He used the robot's hands to grab an old vase and put it in a basket for the trip back to the surface. Khatib explains that the robot and human operator enhance each other's abilities. "The two bring together an amazing synergy. The human and robot can do things in areas too dangerous for a human, while the human is still there."[40] Khatib hopes that OceanOne will eventually be deployed to help scientists study coral reefs that thrive in parts of the ocean too deep for human divers to safely visit.

> "We should regard our robotic probes as scouts that tell us what lies ahead and can go where we yet fear to tread."[41]
>
> —Michael van Pelt, the author of *Space Invaders*

Traveling to distant planets is even more difficult for humans. Yet someday, people may wish or need to settle on worlds other than Earth. Robots will be an essential part of this move, if it ever happens. Most likely, robots would first explore worlds to find out if they are habitable. Then they would set up and build the structures humans need before any settlers arrive. Michael van Pelt, the author of *Space Invaders*, writes, "We should regard our robotic probes as scouts that tell us what lies ahead and can go where we yet fear to tread."[41]

For now, robotic space probes mainly gather scientific data. The two robots rolling around right now on Mars—Opportunity and Curiosity—regularly send photos and other data back to Earth. Thanks to their investigations, scientists now know that liquid water once flowed on Mars. This means the planet may have once held life. A pair of very early robotic spacecraft, Voyager 1 and 2, have flown past many planets, gathering valuable data. Voyager 1 left the solar system in 2012. This robot is humanity's first and only ambassador to the universe beyond the small pocket of space surrounding the sun. These robotic voyagers have given humanity a new perspective on what it means to live on Earth. It is really just a tiny planet in the midst of a vast universe.

CHAPTER 4

Robots vs. Humanity

As robots take on more and different types of jobs, some people are growing uneasy. They worry about robots replacing humans. From some perspectives, it is reasonable to feel concerned. Between 1990 and 2007, every new industrial robot led to the loss of between three and six jobs for humans, according to a study by the National Bureau of Economic Research. The machines ousted people with routine, manual jobs, such as assembly line workers, transport workers, and machinists. The same study also concluded that adding robots to the economy lowers wages for humans. That is because the cost of work becomes cheaper overall. Humans must compete with robots for the same type of job.

Experts disagree on what these facts mean for the future of the world economy and society. Some believe that the economy will adjust and people will find new ways to contribute. After all, new technologies have always changed the job market, and people have continued to find employment and have been able to work. Others worry that this time will be different. They think that robots and computer systems will become too good at too many jobs and will perhaps lead to an economic collapse.

New Technology Creates New Opportunities

From the printing press to the automobile to the personal computer, new inventions eliminate the need for certain jobs. For example, the personal computer rapidly replaced workers who performed basic arithmetic and other calculations. However, new inventions also lead to the creation of new jobs. For example, many people devote their entire careers to engineering computer technology, writing software for computers, and doing other jobs that did not exist just a few decades ago.

Although a factory that installs a welding robot, for example, would no longer need to hire human welders, it would still need people who install, maintain, and repair welding robots. Vint Cerf, a vice president at Google, says, "Historically, technology has created more jobs than it destroys and there is no reason to think otherwise in this case. Someone has to make and service all these advanced devices."[42] Often, a new technology creates entire new industries that are difficult to imagine ahead of time. In economics, this trend is known as creative destruction.

Although robotic technology has made some jobs previously performed by humans obsolete, it has also created new types of jobs, including robot maintenance. Here, a mechanic repairs a robot.

Advances in robotics increase the overall productivity of the economy. A company that can produce more items for less money can lower the price of those items. This will likely increase the number of items it sells, which should generate more profit and allow the company to expand and hire more employees. In addition, the general public also benefits from access to cheaper goods and services. Ideally, the workers who are displaced along the way will find jobs in other higher-paying fields. For this reason, US treasury secretary Steven Mnuchin is not worried about robots taking away Americans' jobs. "Quite frankly, I'm optimistic," he says. "We need to invest in training, we need to invest in education."[43]

Retraining workers to take on more skilled jobs can lead to success. Consider Matt Zeigler, who started out as a welder at a factory in Indiana. When his company purchased a robotic welder, he began spending his breaks learning as much as he could about the new technology. He eventually became a top robot programmer at Motomon, a robotics company in Ohio. Mnuchin and others believe that robotics technology will create better jobs for people—jobs that are more creative and less repetitive.

> "Historically, technology has created more jobs than it destroys and there is no reason to think otherwise in this case. Someone has to make and service all these advanced devices."[42]
>
> —Vint Cerf, a vice president at Google

Robots, Robots, Everywhere

Not everyone believes that advances in robotics will change the economy, or society, for the better. Some experts caution that robots could take over too much of the economy, too quickly, leading to massive unemployment. It may seem that jobs involving manual labor are in most danger of automation, but that is not the case. Advances in AI have led to the emergence of software that can quickly master jobs for which humans spend years training. For example, software programs can now interpret medical images, which is normally the job of highly educated radiologists. Computers can also diagnose cancer, write engaging articles about sporting events, and produce original music. As these advances continue, robots may soon be employed in nearly every industry.

In many professions, computers and robots will continue to function alongside human workers. For example, Watson, a cancer-diagnosing AI program, already assists human doctors. But the doctor is still the one to interface with the patient. Similarly, pill-picking robot pharmacists free up human pharmacists to spend more time with patients, discussing their medications. Still, automation is likely to reduce the number of humans needed in many professions. For example, at one hospital, a team of seven pharmacy technicians used to fill prescriptions under the supervision of three to four pharmacists. Now, just two technicians work with robots to do the same work. In this case, the other people did not lose their jobs. Instead, they took on new tasks. But there may not always be new tasks around to keep the displaced workers employed.

In his book *Rise of the Robots*, Martin Ford predicts that in the United States, the customer service industry will be most affected by robotics and automation—and soon. Self-serve automatic kiosks will likely replace many stores and restaurants. Some stores will employ robots such as Pepper to assist shoppers. Robots could also replace food servers and cooks. The company Momentum Machines has produced a robot that cranks out hamburgers. It cooks and assembles four hundred of them in an hour. Right now, the fast food industry acts as a safety net for many people who cannot find work elsewhere. If these jobs become scarce, the working class may face an extreme job shortage. Not everyone will be able to get the training and education needed to find work, especially if high-skilled and creative jobs become more automated as well.

Preparing for a Jobless Future

Just because a job *can* be automated, however, does not mean it *will* be. It will likely take a very long time before restaurants decide that automatic burger machines are the best solution. In addition,

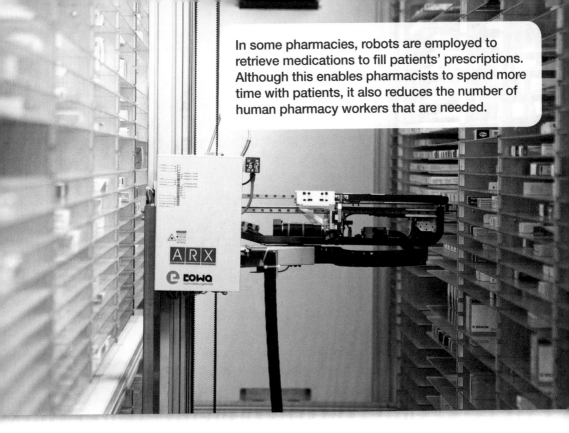

In some pharmacies, robots are employed to retrieve medications to fill patients' prescriptions. Although this enables pharmacists to spend more time with patients, it also reduces the number of human pharmacy workers that are needed.

some customers may decide that they are willing to pay more for a burger made by a human chef. Furthermore, robotics technology requires a big up-front investment in expensive machinery. Switching an industry over to a new way of doing business is a long, slow process. "We have more time than we think to adjust to the world that technology makes possible,"[44] says Matthew J. Slaughter, an economist at Dartmouth College.

As another example, self-driving vehicles are already capable of driving people from one place to another in a city. In fact, the ride company Uber rolled out self-driving cars in Pittsburgh, Pennsylvania, in 2016 to test functionality, map roads, and perform other functions. However, the new technology is extremely expensive. Plus, the rules and regulations for cars that do not have drivers still need to be worked out. Also, a lot of people simply are not comfortable hopping into self-driving cars. So for now, taxi drivers and human Uber drivers still have jobs.

Also, society may work out a way to make a mostly jobless future something to look forward to. In a perfect world, robots

Robot-Proof Jobs

Some jobs are essentially robot proof—at least, for now. It is still extremely difficult to make a robot that handles unpredictable environments, exhibits creativity, or makes judgment calls. Here are a few jobs that robots will not take over any time soon.

Tree pruner: Robots may be good at manual labor, but trees are highly unpredictable structures, and pruning takes place in all sorts of different environments.

Police officer: Police work with robots to handle dangerous situations and analyze crime scene evidence. But human instincts are still required to make tricky judgment calls and solve complex crimes.

Athlete: Some people do watch robot-versus-robot soccer matches, but mainstream sports are about watching the world's strongest, fastest, most agile people accomplish amazing things.

Entrepreneur: Starting a business requires creativity, adaptability, judgment, and leadership. In the near future, humans will be the only ones starting and leading new businesses, though they may get lots of help from robotic assistants along the way.

Robot maintenance worker: Until robots can fix themselves, humans still need to install, maintain, and repair the machines.

and intelligent software would free people from almost all labor, leaving them free to pursue whatever creative, fun, and interesting things they want. In this type of world, the government might provide a universal basic income, like an allowance for every adult. This is not a new concept; the philosopher Bertrand Russell promoted the idea in 1918. But robots may make this kind of social support system necessary.

A New Kind of Being

The idea of robot cooks, drivers, and more makes some people uneasy for a very different reason. They worry about a growing lack of human connection. Technology already makes it all too easy to send an e-mail or text instead of stopping by to deliver a message in person. Once robots start taking on more customer service roles, daily interactions with other human beings will become even less common.

Perhaps it is not such a terrible thing to not have to talk to a person while ordering a burger or buying a shirt. But robots are also poised to eventually take on teaching, nursing, and caretaker roles. These jobs require a lot of face-to-face interaction. Many people become friends with their teachers and nurses. Experts are not sure what it would mean to be friends with a robot. "How do we build relationships with what is essentially a new kind of being?"[45] asks journalist Matt Simon in an article for *Wired* magazine.

Robots of all kinds already inspire empathy in people. At the DARPA Robotics Challenge, spectators gasped when robots fell and cheered when they succeeded. Gill Pratt, the organizer of the competition, said, "Ordinary people, not roboticists, felt this identity, sympathy, empathy for the robot. The thrill of victory, the agony of defeat."[46] Even the vacuum cleaner Roomba has touched peoples' lives. Perhaps due to the fact that the robot moves around like an animal, many owners seem to treat it more like a pet than an appliance. They often give names to their robots. Colin Angle, one of the cofounders of iRobot, named his robot vacuum Roswell. Many owners occasionally talk to the machine, just like they might talk to a dog or cat, even though they realize it does not understand. Some grow so attached to their robot that they cannot imagine replacing it. Angle recalls one woman who called his company's support line soon after Roomba launched. He suggested she send her broken Roomba back for a replacement, and she said, "No, I'm not sending you Rosie."[47]

These relationships only go one way, of course. A Roomba is not capable of having feelings for its owner. But some social

> "Ordinary people, not roboticists, felt this identity, sympathy, empathy for the robot. The thrill of victory, the agony of defeat."[46]
>
> —Gill Pratt, the organizer of the DARPA Robotics Challenge

robots are designed to exhibit emotions. The machines cannot really feel happy or confused, but they can move their faces or change their voices in ways that seem to convey human emotions. Engineers are also designing robots with soft or flexible bodies. These developments further blur the line between machine and living creature.

Missing the Human Touch

Several companies have developed robot pets in the form of cats, dogs, seals, and other cuddly creatures. Researchers at the Massachusetts Institute of Technology are developing a robot they call Huggable. It is a teddy bear that responds to touch. A specialist can talk to a child using a microphone inside the bear. The team hopes that Huggable will help kids in the hospital feel less lonely, bored, and scared.

Other social robots connect with people through artificial intelligence that allows them to converse in human languages or express emotions through gestures and tone. For example, the Nao

Meet Paro

The robot known as Paro resembles a baby harp seal. It was designed as a medical device to help calm and comfort elderly people suffering from dementia. Research has shown that interacting with live animals helps reduce symptoms of depression and relieve chronic pain. But live animals need constant care and may scratch, bite, or cause allergies. A robotic pet avoids the drawbacks of live animals and seems to provide many of the same benefits.

Geoffrey Lane is a psychologist who introduced a Paro robot into the veterans' hospital in Livermore, California. "People are able to connect with this robot," he says. "It's designed to behave in a way and interact with the person so that you want to touch it, you want to pet it. . . . [People] have the same reaction that they do to any other cute animal or cute baby." Kathy Craig, one of the therapists at the hospital, adds, "A lot of them think it's real."

Quoted in Angela Johnston, "Robotic Seals Comfort Dementia Patients but Raise Ethical Concerns," KALW Local Public Radio, August 17, 2015. http://kalw.org.

robot can hunch its shoulders to show sadness or lift its arms for a hug. Pepper can tell if a person's face is sad or angry. It reacts to that emotion with comfort or concern. Steve Carlin, the vice president of SoftBank Robotics America, says that Pepper was designed to make people want to interact with it. "Its height, shape, the fact that it has arms that can gesticulate—are all designed to show empathy,"[48] he says.

Some experts are disturbed by the idea of people connecting with robots, especially when they are children or elderly adults who may not understand that the robot is not a real being. Empathetic robots could trick vulnerable people into caring about something that will never care back. Ken Goldberg, a roboticist at the University of California, Berkeley, says, "I don't believe in companion robots. . . . If I'm lonely, the last thing I want is a robot to come in and somehow be my friend. That's even more depressing."[49] Goldberg and many others feel that it is just not possible for a robot to provide an appropriate level of care and support to people who need it. "Nothing can take the place of human touch, eye contact, warmth, reminiscence, presence, compassion and empathy—bearing one another's burdens through real relationships,"[50] says Daniel C. Potts, a doctor and the director at Dementia Dynamics, a company that trains caregivers.

Unfortunately, real people and real pets are not always available to offer real caring. "A reliable robot may be better than an unreliable or abusive person, or than no one at all,"[51] says Louise Aronson, an expert in elder care at the University of California, San Francisco. She has cared for many elderly patients and imagines that their lives could only be improved if they had a companion robot. Aronson contends that even if the robot's responses are not real, its conversation and interaction may be better than nothing.

> "I don't believe in companion robots. . . . If I'm lonely, the last thing I want is a robot to come in and somehow be my friend. That's even more depressing."[49]
>
> —Ken Goldberg, a roboticist at the University of California, Berkeley

Becoming Cyborgs

As robots become more and more human-like in their ability to provide companionship, real people are also becoming more robotic. A smartphone or other digital device is like a portable robotic brain that instantly offers up knowledge and connection, often through a digital personality such as Siri or Alexa. People are so dependent on these devices that they often feel anxious, bored, or incomplete if they try to give them up for an extended period. It is as if they have lost a part of themselves.

Other robotic devices literally become part of the body. Paralyzed people can be fitted with an exoskeleton, which is a robotic suit that makes lifeless legs or arms move and support weight. For example, in 2014 robotics helped Stacey Kozel hike the Appalachian Trail. Kozel, who is paralyzed from the waist down, used an exoskeleton to complete the journey. Robotics can also help people who have lost a limb and often wear a device called a prosthetic. Today's prosthetics incorporate advanced robotics technology. Doctors can link a robotic arm or leg to a patient's own nerves, allowing the person to control the limb with his or her brain. Jesse Sullivan, a man who lost both of his arms in an electrical accident, received the first mind-controlled robotic limbs in 2001. He says that controlling the devices is simple: "All I have to do is want to do it, and I do it."[52] Today researchers are even beginning to give robotic devices the ability to send sensations back to the user's brain. That means people such as Sullivan could soon feel sensations such as holding hands. Implants connected to the brain can also help restore hearing to the deaf and basic sight to the blind.

Exoskeletons and prosthetics help people with disabilities participate more fully in the world. Someday, though, these sorts of devices may be used to enhance normal people's abilities. In comic books, the superhero Iron Man wears a suit that enhances his strength and speed and provides other amazing abilities. Several companies around the world are developing or selling exoskeletons intended to allow human workers or soldiers to lift very heavy loads without much effort.

One exciting use of robotic technology is to aid people with disabilities by fitting them with devices that essentially become part of the human body. Here, army veteran Carrie Krischke uses a robotic arm to retrieve a mug from her kitchen cupboard.

A person whose robotic body parts give him or her abilities beyond what a normal person would have is called a cyborg. In the future, regular people may choose to modify their bodies and minds to become smarter, stronger, or faster. This could create a distinct class division between people who can afford the enhancements and those who cannot. A real-life Iron Man could easily take advantage of normal humans. But this type of troubling situation is still a long way off because bionic parts are not yet functional enough for healthy people to get much benefit from using them routinely.

It is impossible to foresee exactly how robots will affect human employment, relationships, or even human bodies. But no matter what happens, humans will have to get used to life with robots. Smart machines will increasingly become a part of people's daily lives, leading to changes in how they interact with technology and with each other. The rise of the robots may lead people to change their minds about what it means to be human and what it means to be a machine.

CHAPTER 5

Heroes or Overlords?

Robots are making human lives easier, safer, and more interesting. People continue to develop robotics and AI because the benefits are so amazing. Robotics technology increases the overall productivity of society. It also enhances human abilities in many realms, including science, engineering, and medicine. It is impossible to know exactly how robotics will alter peoples' lives decades or centuries from now. But given the rapid increases in computing power over the past century, it seems likely that robotics technology will continue to improve.

Be Anywhere, Anytime

Thanks to the Internet, it is already possible to connect instantly to people around the world through text, speech, and video. Likewise, virtual reality technology adds the ability to experience even more sensations in the digital realm, including touch and 360-degree vision. Robotics could bring these virtual connections into mainstream everyday life. Consider a robot that could act as someone's avatar. The person would sit at home and use a virtual reality device to operate a robot as it walked around the real world. The human operator would experience sights, sounds, touch sensations, and perhaps even smells and tastes through the robot's sensors.

Current telepresence robots only offer the ability to see, hear, speak, and move around in a limited area. But in the future, inhabiting a robot could feel almost like walking around in a regular human body. Businesspeople and students have already used telepresence technology to go to work or school without leaving home. In the future, this could be what everyone does every day. The technology could also be used for travel. For example, in 2016 journalist Evan Ackerman used a telepresence robot to visit the Oregon Zoo in Portland. He reports that the experience was interesting but a little unnerving since he was disembodied. If someone had tried to grab the robot, he could not have done anything about it. So family members who were there in person escorted him around. Yet he imagines that the technology could be a lot more fun in the future, once the robot body is more capable and independent. "You could decide 'Hey, I want to wander around Singapore today,' and you just get off the couch, get on the computer and log in, and suddenly you're in a robot," he says. "You can go explore Singapore."[53]

> "You just get off the couch, get on the computer and log in, and suddenly you're in a robot. You can go explore Singapore."[53]
>
> —Evan Ackerman, a contributing editor at *IEEE Spectrum* magazine

When people do need to travel, a robot will likely be the one to bring them to their destination. Self-driving cars are robots that are poised to dramatically reduce the number of car accidents and the amount of traffic. Such cars will likely be able to communicate with each other to plan, as a group, the most efficient way for each car to get to its destination. The cars will also give people more time during the day. Time formerly spent driving could instead be spent working, reading, or talking to friends and family. In addition, a world with a lot of self-driving cars would likely be a world in which very few people owned their own vehicle. Instead, they may increasingly rely on self-driving taxis or co-own cars

A woman reads a magazine behind the wheel of a self-driving car. The cars will give people more free time during the day because riders can work, read, or talk on the phone instead of having to pay attention to the road.

with groups of people. This would make the entire transportation system much more efficient and better for the environment.

Make Anything

In addition to transforming travel, robots will continue to change the manufacturing industry. Despite the prevalence of robots in this area, there is plenty of room for improvement. Older factory robots have no ability to sense obstacles in their path. For this reason, they can be very dangerous. An industrial robot arm will not stop its work if a human gets in the way. Moreover, these robots are very expensive to install and program. These limitations have prevented many smaller factories and manufacturers from using robots. But a new generation of manufacturing robots—called collaborative robots, or cobots for short—work safely alongside people. They do not need special programming; instead, a person with no training can move the robot's arm to show it what to do.

Rodney Brooks, the cofounder of iRobot, has also started another company, Rethink Robotics, to make collaborative robots. Brooks predicts that smart cobots will revolutionize manufacturing. "We will see a change in manufacturing into more local, smaller-scale operations, but manufacturing very complex things,"[54] he says.

Two technologies closely related to robotics—nanotechnology and 3-D printing—could transform manufacturing even more dramatically. Nanotechnology deals with the manipulation of atoms or molecules, and 3-D printing involves the manufacture of solid objects by squirting or molding base material according to a computer model. A combination of robotics with either of these two technologies could allow factories to become much smaller and to construct complex objects on command. People could have small factories at home that churn out the items they need. Some companies are already setting up 3-D printing farms, which are

The Gray Goo

It is a nightmare scenario: tiny robots that can assemble anything, including more of themselves, go out of control. They take apart everything in their path—including people, animals, and plants—in a never-ending quest to make more and more tiny robots. Eventually, they consume the entire Earth. This doomsday story first appeared in a 1986 book by Eric Drexler, a pioneer in the field of nanotechnology. Drexler called the mass of devouring robots "grey goo."

The grey goo makes a great science fiction story, but it is not likely to happen. "Runaway replication would only be the product of a deliberate and difficult engineering process, not an accident," says Chris Phoenix of the Center for Responsible Nanotechnology. However, the ability to manufacture anything very quickly is still a cause for concern. For example, he warns that people could use such technology to make huge quantities of weapons.

Quoted in Phys.org, "Nanotechnology Pioneer Slays 'Grey Goo' Myths," June 11, 2004. https://phys.org.

like factories that run without any humans on site. Roboticist Hans Moravec imagines how a world with instant manufacturing might work. "Humans may be able to live in uncluttered spaces," he says. "Robots could construct needed items, even food or housing, on the spot, or assemble them from nearby caches. Items no longer needed could be disassembled back to raw materials."[55]

Nanotechnology combined with robotics could also lead to exciting advances in medicine. Cell-sized robots could patrol the body, seeking out disease and making repairs. "The [technology's] first real application will be in treating cancers,"[56] predicts Dr. Sylvain Martel, the director of the NanoRobotics Laboratory at the École Polytechnique de Montréal in Canada. Tiny robots could deliver cancer-killing drugs only to a cancerous tumor, leaving healthy cells alone. Eventually, surgery could become obsolete as these microscopic machines repair problems from the inside.

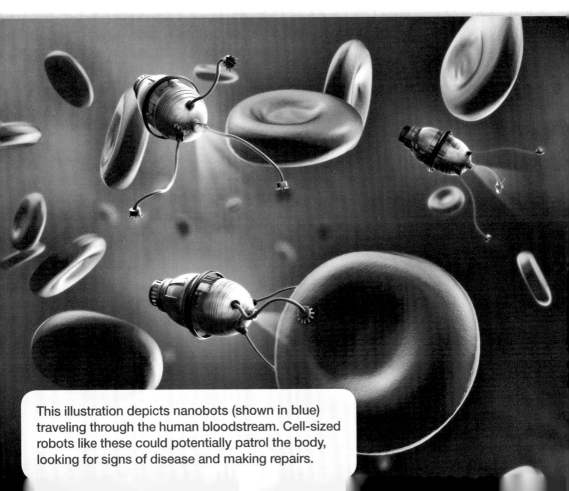

This illustration depicts nanobots (shown in blue) traveling through the human bloodstream. Cell-sized robots like these could potentially patrol the body, looking for signs of disease and making repairs.

Extinction

Robotics technology could save lives, but it could also destroy them. The killer robot villains of numerous science fiction stories could one day become reality, though they are not likely to resemble the battle droids in *Star Wars*. More likely, an autonomous weapon would be a guided missile system or a drone so tiny that it fits in the palm of a hand. These types of weapons could hunt down and kill a specific target. Or they could target anyone fitting certain criteria, making it possible to use an army of flying robots to commit genocide from a distance. If a country or organization wanted to develop such weapons, it could potentially do so in a matter of years, warn AI experts. "[The technology] is easier to achieve than self-driving cars, which require far higher standards of performance,"[57] says Stuart Russell, an AI scientist at the University of California, Berkeley.

Russell and Max Tegmark, the cofounder of the Future of Life Institute, an organization that works to ensure that AI research is conducted safely, coauthored a 2017 letter calling for a ban on autonomous weapons. More than one hundred AI experts signed the letter, which stated, "Once developed, lethal autonomous weapons will permit armed conflict to be fought at a scale greater than ever, and at timescales faster than humans can comprehend. These can be weapons of terror, weapons that despots and terrorists use against innocent populations, and weapons hacked to behave in undesirable ways."[58]

Killer robots would bring about catastrophe only if people unleash them on each other. AI poses a subtler danger. A computer program could potentially become much more intelligent than humans. Many AI programs can already write new software or modify their own software. If a program is designed to continually write better, smarter AI, it could very rapidly become extremely intelligent—and it would most likely be impossible for humans to control the actions of such an entity. To understand why, think about a flock of crows. The birds are quite smart. Most humans have no desire to get rid of them completely. But if people needed a new highway, they would be unlikely to halt construction to save one tree where some crows live. Human intelligence has enabled control of the environment. No other animal can stop humans from making progress towards their goals. Machine intelligence, however, could control life in ways that are impossible to imagine with human brains. A sufficiently intelligent computer with access to the Internet could control enough machines around the world to build whatever it needs to accomplish its goals. Any humans who got in the way would seem as insignificant as a flock of crows.

Entrepreneur and inventor Elon Musk, whose company Tesla makes a self-driving car, has warned that AI is potentially more dangerous than nuclear weapons. He compares the development of AI to fictional stories about sorcerers who summon demons. In these stories, the human always thinks he can control the demon and force it to do his bidding. But that never works out. The demon is just too powerful. "With artificial intelligence we are summoning the demon,"[59] says Musk. He and others warn that humans are building something that may be too powerful to control.

Live Happily Ever After

Some experts, however, are more excited than worried about the prospect of robotic intelligence. They believe that if extremely intelligent robots could be controlled with some system akin to Asimov's Three Laws of Robotics, then these nightmare scenarios could be prevented. A community of AI researchers has come up with a list of principles that will help ensure the safety of future AI and robotics. One such principle states that "humans should choose how and whether to delegate decisions to AI systems, to accomplish human-chosen objectives."[60] Thanks to the fact that so many researchers are now seriously working on AI safety, Tegmark says, "I'm feeling more optimistic about the future of life than I have in a long time."[61]

A powerful artificial intelligence program potentially could solve any problem that humans face. One such use might be to protect against climate change or natural disasters such as wildfires.

A sufficiently powerful and well-controlled AI program could conceivably solve any problem. For example, AI could potentially invent technology to protect the planet from threats such as climate change or natural disasters. It could also revolutionize medicine to the point where dying becomes an extremely rare event. In addition, it could come up with ways to feed and house all those immortal people on Earth or even on other planets. These people of the future may not have to work. They may live out their lives as they please while robot servants supply everything they need. Moravec imagines that "there will be robotic playmates, virtual realities, and personalized works of art that stir the emotions like nothing before . . . [as well as] luxury visits to almost anywhere, and things yet unimagined."[62]

"There will be robotic playmates, virtual realities, and personalized works of art that stir the emotions like nothing before."[62]

—Hans Moravec, a roboticist at Carnegie Mellon University

Merging with Machines

In both the killer robot and the hero robot scenarios, however, there is a fundamental assumption being made: that both robots and humans will exist as separate beings. Some experts believe that this assumption is flawed. They think robots and humans will gradually merge together. In this vision of the future, superintelligent beings will conquer the universe. They will be people who have enhanced their bodies and minds with robotics and other technology. "We will become a merger between flesh and machines,"[63] predicts Brooks. Moravec and computer scientist and futurist Ray Kurzweil are two of the biggest supporters of this idea. Kurzweil believes that advances in robotics, genetics, and nanotechnology will make this merger possible. He says, "By understanding the information processes underlying life, we are starting to learn to reprogram our biology to achieve the virtual elimination of disease, dramatic expansion of human potential, and radical life extension."[64]

> "We will become a merger between flesh and machines."[63]
>
> —Rodney Brooks, the cofounder of iRobot and Rethink Robotics

The end point of this type of engineered evolution is impossible to imagine. Moravec calls human/robot beings "Exes" and predicts that they will colonize the universe. He thinks that they might be able to morph their bodies into whatever shape makes the most sense for the job at hand, potentially resembling "spiders, bugs, pogo sticks, snakes, blimps, cars, barrels, power shovels." He goes on to say, "An Ex may often be surrounded by an illuminated cloud that does its bidding as if by magic."[65] Some experts have suggested that humans may one day download their minds onto computers, allowing them to live forever either as disembodied souls or in a succession of bodies.

These bizarre and marvelous ideas are part of an extremely distant future that many believe is just wishful thinking. "We are a long, long way from being able to download ourselves into com-

When Robots Rule the Road

Human error causes around 90 percent of car accidents, according to a number of different studies. Therefore, many are looking to self-driving cars to dramatically increase the safety of the roads. "There is compelling logic in removing humans—the key source of the error—from the driving equation," says Hussein Dia, a civil engineer at Swinburne University of Technology who specializes in self-driving vehicles. "Driven by artificial intelligence, these vehicles will not make errors of judgement the way a human driver does. They will not drink and drive. They will not fall asleep behind the wheel. They will not get distracted by playing Pokémon Go."

However, self-driving cars will not be perfect. Machines have their share of problems. Software glitches or designer oversights could cause accidents. Still, most experts agree that a world without human drivers would be a safer place.

Quoted in Phys.org, "Self-Driving Cars Could Dramatically Reduce the Road Toll," September 26, 2017. https://phys.org.

puters or robots,"[66] acknowledges Brooks. Steven Pinker, a psychologist, says that "there is not the slightest reason" to believe that technology will lead to eternal life. "The fact that you can visualize a future in your imagination is not evidence that it is likely or even possible,"[67] he explains.

One point remains uncontroversial: robotics technology is dramatically changing what it means to be human. Robots are altering how people work, play, learn, and even how long they live. They are changing our planet and our universe. It remains to be seen whether these changes will eventually make the world a better place to live.

SOURCE NOTES

Introduction: Venturing Out into the Universe

1. Michael van Pelt, *Space Invaders*. New York: Springer, 2007, p. 20.
2. Quoted in Tomasz Nowakowski, "NASA Counting on Humanoid Robots in Deep Space Exploration," Phys.org, January 26, 2016. https://phys.org.
3. Bill Gates, "A Robot in Every Home," *Scientific American*, January 1, 2007. www.scientificamerican.com.
4. Quoted in Mark Honigsbaum, "Meet the New Generation of Robots. They're Almost Human . . . ," *Guardian* (Manchester, UK), September 15, 2013. www.theguardian.com.

Chapter One: From Fiction to Factories

5. Isaac Asimov, *I, Robot*. New York: Random House, 2004, p. 184.
6. Asimov, *I, Robot*, p. 77.
7. T.R. Kennedy Jr., "Electronic Computer Flashes Answers, May Speed Engineering," *New York Times*, February 15, 1946. www.nytimes.com.
8. Norbert Wiener, *The Human Use of Human Beings: Cybernetics and Society*. New York: Da Capo, 1988, p. 16.
9. Quoted in Wiener, *The Human Use of Human Beings*, p. 174.
10. Quoted in Philip Welch, "Letters," *London Review of Books*, vol. 34, no. 19, October 11, 2012. www.lrb.co.uk.
11. Quoted in Emily Langer, "Joseph F. Engelberger, Pioneer of Robotics, Dies at 90," *Washington Post*, December 4, 2015. www.washingtonpost.com.
12. Quoted in Langer, "Joseph F. Engelberger, Pioneer of Robotics, Dies at 90."

13. Quoted in Tekla S. Perry, "SRI's Pioneering Mobile Robot Shakey Honored as IEEE Milestone," *IEEE Spectrum*, February 17, 2017. http://spectrum.ieee.org.
14. Quoted in Harry Henderson, *Modern Robotics*. New York: Chelsea House, 2006, p. 32.
15. Quoted in Larry Elliott, "Robots Will Not Lead to Fewer Jobs—but the Hollowing Out of the Middle Class," *Guardian* (Manchester, UK), August 20, 2017. www.theguardian.com.
16. Quoted in *Verge*, "The 2015 DARPA Robotics Challenge Finals," YouTube, June 12, 2015. www.youtube.com.

Chapter Two: At Your Service

17. Quoted in Nick Wingfield, "As Amazon Pushes Forward with Robots, Workers Find New Roles," *New York Times*, September 10, 2017. www.nytimes.com.
18. Quoted in Tanya M. Anandan, "The Business of Automation, Betting on Robots," *Robotics Industry Insights*, May 19, 2016. www.robotics.org.
19. Quoted in Nick Summers, "Shropshire Farm Completes Harvest with Nothing but Robots," *Engadget* (blog), September 7, 2017. www.engadget.com.
20. Quoted in Sandra Blakeslee, "A Robot Arm Assists in 3 Brain Operations," *New York Times*, June 25, 1985. www.nytimes.com.
21. Quoted in Gina Kolata, "Results Unproven, Robotic Surgery Wins Converts," *New York Times*, February 13, 2010. www.nytimes.com.
22. Quoted in Simon Parkin, "The Tiny Robots Revolutionizing Eye Surgery," *MIT Technology Review*, January 19, 2017. www.technologyreview.com.
23. Quoted in Chris Gordon, "Robot Allows Maryland Boy with Degenerative Disease to Attend School, Connect with Classmates," NBC Washington, March 24, 2017. www.nbcwashington.com.
24. Quoted in Henderson, *Modern Robotics*, p. 55.
25. Quoted in Sam Byford, "Sony Just Announced a New Aibo Robot Dog," *Verge*, October 31, 2017. www.theverge.com.
26. Quoted in Meaghan Meehan, "Robots and Technology Reign as the Toy Industry Prepares for 2017," Blasting News, October 6, 2016. http://us.blastingnews.com.

27. Quoted in Matthew J. Stock, "British Robot Helping Autistic Children with Their Social Skills," Reuters, March 31, 2017. www.reuters.com.
28. Quoted in Voice of America, "Robot Helps Children with Disabilities," December 11, 2009. www.voanews.com.
29. Quoted in Robert McGarvey, "There Is a Perilous Shortage of Elder Caregivers," TheStreet, March 23, 2017. www.thestreet.com.
30. Quoted in Maija Palmer, "SoftBank Puts Faith in Future of Robots," *Financial Times*, March 11, 2012. www.ft.com.

Chapter Three: Disasters, Wars, and Exploration

31. Quoted in Leander Kahney, "Robots Scour WTC Wreckage," *Wired*, September 18, 2001. www.wired.com.
32. Robin Murphy, "These Robots Come to the Rescue After a Disaster," TEDWomen 2015, May 2015. www.ted.com.
33. Quoted in Associated Press, "New Robots Well Trained for War," NBC News, January 14, 2003. www.nbcnews.com.
34. Quoted in Cheryl Pellerin, "Robots Could Save Soldiers' Lives, Army General Says," US Department of Defense, August 17, 2011. http://archive.defense.gov.
35. Quoted in Caroline Rees, "Cherokee Nation Technologies Supports NOAA/NASA UAS Hurricane Forecasting," Unmanned Systems Technology, November 9, 2016. www.unmannedsystemstechnology.com.
36. Quoted in Deborah Findling and Jeniece Pettitt, "How Firefighters Are Using Drones to Save Lives," CNBC, August 27, 2017. www.cnbc.com.
37. Quoted in John Lauritsen, "Drone Helps Rochester Police Find Missing 84-Year-Old Man," CBS Minnesota, November 6, 2017. http://minnesota.cbslocal.com.
38. Quoted in Nina Strochlic, "The Surprising Ways Drones Are Saving Lives," *National Geographic*, June 2017. www.nationalgeographic.com.
39. Murphy, "These Robots Come to the Rescue After a Disaster."
40. Quoted in Bjorn Carey, "Maiden Voyage of Stanford's Humanoid Robotic Diver Recovers Treasures from King Louis XIV's Wrecked Flagship," *Stanford News*, April 27, 2016. https://news.stanford.edu.
41. Van Pelt, *Space Invaders*, pp. 20–21.

Chapter Four: Robots vs. Humanity

42. Quoted in Aaron Smith and Janna Anderson, "AI, Robotics, and the Future of Jobs," Pew Research Center, August 6, 2014. www.pewinternet.org.

43. Quoted in Adi Robertson, "Treasury Secretary 'Not at All' Worried About Robots Taking Jobs," *Verge*, March 24, 2017. www.theverge.com.

44. Quoted in Steve Lohr, "Robots Will Take Jobs, but Not as Fast as Some Fear, New Report Says," *New York Times*, January 12, 2017. www.nytimes.com.

45. Matt Simon, "Companion Robots Are Here, Just Don't Fall in Love with Them," *Wired*, August 2, 2017. www.wired.com.

46. Quoted in Evan Ackerman and Erico Guizzo, "DARPA Robotics Challenge: Amazing Moments, Lessons Learned, and What's Next," *IEEE Spectrum*, June 11, 2015. https://spectrum.ieee.org.

47. Quoted in Celeste Biever, "My Roomba's Name Is Roswell," *Slate*, March 23, 2014. www.slate.com.

48. Quoted in April Glaser, "Pepper, the Emotional Robot, Learns to Feel Like an American," *Wired*, June 7, 2017. www.wired.com.

49. Quoted in Matt Simon, "The Genesis of Kuri, the Friendly Home Robot," *Wired*, November 30, 2017. www.wired.com.

50. Quoted in Carol Bradley Bursack, "I, Caregiver: Do Robots Have a Place in Elder Care?," AgingCare.com, 2014. www.agingcare.com.

51. Louise Aronson, "The Future of Robot Caregivers," *New York Times*, July 19, 2014. www.nytimes.com.

52. Quoted in Keith Oppenheim, "Jesse Sullivan Powers Robotic Arms with His Mind," CNN, March 23, 2006. www.cnn.com.

Chapter Five: Heroes or Overlords?

53. Quoted in Julia Franz, "Need to Be in Two Places at Once? Try a Telepresence Robot," PRI, October 1, 2016. www.pri.org.

54. Quoted in Michael Chui, "Robots Mean Business: A Conversation with Rodney Brooks," McKinsey & Company, February 2014. www.mckinsey.com.

55. Hans Moravec, *Robot: Mere Machine to Transcendent Mind*. New York: Oxford University Press, 1999, p. 138.

56. Quoted in Jenna Kainic, "Microbots: Using Nanotechnology in Medicine," *Yale Scientific*, February 5, 2013. www.yale scientific.org.

57. Quoted in Ian Sample, "Ban on Killer Robots Urgently Needed, Say Scientists," *Guardian* (Manchester, UK), November 12, 2017. www.theguardian.com.

58. Quoted in Samuel Gibbs, "Elon Musk Leads 116 Experts Calling for Outright Ban of Killer Robots," *Guardian* (Manchester, UK), August 20, 2017. www.theguardian.com.

59. Quoted in Samuel Gibbs, "Elon Musk: Artificial Intelligence Is Our Biggest Existential Threat," *Guardian* (Manchester, UK), October 27, 2014. www.theguardian.com.

60. Max Tegmark, *Life 3.0: Being Human in the Age of Artificial Intelligence*. New York: Knopf, 2017, p. 331.

61. Tegmark, *Life 3.0*, p. 332.

62. Moravec, *Robot*, p. 141.

63. Rodney Brooks, *Flesh and Machines: How Robots Will Change Us*. New York: Pantheon, 2002, p. x.

64. Quoted in Sveta McShane and Jason Dorrier, "Ray Kurzweil Predicts Three Technologies Will Define Our Future," SingularityHub, April 19, 2016. https://singularityhub.com.

65. Moravec, *Robot*, p. 150.

66. Brooks, *Flesh and Machines*, p. 208.

67. Quoted in Martin Ford, *Rise of the Robots: Technology and the Threat of a Jobless Future*. New York: Basic Books, 2015, p. 237.

GLOSSARY

artificial intelligence: A machine's ability to perform tasks that usually require human intelligence.

autonomous: Able to act freely and independently.

cyborg: A being with both biological and mechanical body parts.

empathy: The ability to identify with and share another's feelings.

exoskeleton: In robotics, a suit that enhances the wearer's physical abilities.

gesticulate: The act of moving the arms or body to enhance spoken communication.

humanoid: A robot that looks like a person.

logistics: The managment of the details of an operation.

mundane: Boring or ordinary.

nanotechnology: The science of manipulating materials on an extremely small scale.

prosthetic: An artificial arm, hand, leg, or foot.

teleoperation: The act of controlling a robot from a distance.

telepresence: The use of robotics to be virtually present in a distant location.

unmanned aerial vehicles (UAVs): Aircraft that fly without pilots; also called drones.

FOR FURTHER RESEARCH

Books

Erik Brynjolfsson and Andrew McAfee, *The Second Machine Age: Work, Progress, and Prosperity in a Time of Brilliant Technologies*. New York: Norton, 2014.

Paul Dumouchel and Luisa Damiano, *Living with Robots*. Cambridge, MA: Harvard University Press, 2017.

Martin Ford, *Rise of the Robots: Technology and the Threat of a Jobless Future*. New York: Basic Books, 2015.

John Markoff, *Machines of Loving Grace: The Quest for Common Ground Between Humans and Robots*. New York: HarperCollins, 2015.

David Mindell, *Our Robots, Ourselves: Robotics and the Myths of Autonomy*. New York: Viking, 2015.

Internet Sources

Evan Ackerman and Erico Guizzo, "DARPA Robotics Challenge: Amazing Moments, Lessons Learned, and What's Next," *IEEE Spectrum*, June 11, 2015. https://spectrum.ieee.org/automaton/robotics/humanoids/darpa-robotics-challenge-amazing-moments-lessons-learned-whats-next.

Tanya M. Anandan, "The Business of Automation, Betting on Robots," Robotic Industries Association, May 19, 2016. www.robotics.org/content-detail.cfm/Industrial-Robotics-Industry-Insights/The-Business-of-Automation-Betting-on-Robots/content_id/6076.

Deborah Findling and Jeniece Pettitt, "How Firefighters Are Using Drones to Save Lives," CNBC, August 27, 2017. www.cnbc.com/2017/08/26/skyfire-consulting-trains-firefighters-to-use-drones-to-save-lives.html.

Steve Lohr, "Robots Will Take Jobs, but Not as Fast as Some Fear, New Report Says," *New York Times*, January 12, 2017. www.ny times.com/2017/01/12/technology/robots-will-take-jobs-but-not -as-fast-as-some-fear-new-report-says.html.

Robin Murphy, "These Robots Come to the Rescue After a Disaster," TEDWomen 2015, May 2015. www.ted.com/talks/rob in_murphy_these_robots_come_to_the_rescue_after_a_disaster /transcript#t-143112.

Ian Sample, "Ban on Killer Robots Urgently Needed, Say Scientists," *Guardian* (Manchester, UK), November 12, 2017. www.the guardian.com/science/2017/nov/13/ban-on-killer-robots-urgently -needed-say-scientists.

Matt Simon, "Companion Robots Are Here, Just Don't Fall in Love with Them," *Wired*, August 2, 2017. www.wired.com/story /companion-robots-are-here.

Aaron Smith and Janna Anderson, "AI, Robotics, and the Future of Jobs," Pew Research Center, August 6, 2014. www.pewinternet .org/2014/08/06/future-of-jobs.

James Vincent, "Robots Do Destroy Jobs and Lower Wages, Says New Study," *Verge*, March 28, 2017. www.theverge .com/2017/3/28/15086576/robot-jobs-automation-unemployent -us-labor-market.

Websites

Future of Life Institute (https://futureoflife.org). This organization is devoted to ensuring that technological advances are beneficial for humanity as a whole. Artificial intelligence and autonomous weapons are two of the group's main areas of focus.

IEEE Spectrum (https://spectrum.ieee.org/robotics). *IEEE Spectrum* is a magazine and website produced by the IEEE, a professional organization for engineers and scientists. The website contains a section devoted to news about the latest robotics research.

Kurzweil Accelerating Intelligence (www.kurzweilai.net). This website explores new ideas and trends in robotics, electronics, artificial intelligence, biotechnology, and more. The goal of the site is to explore the growth of technologies that are radically changing the world.

Robotic Industries Association (www.robotics.org). This website provides information to help companies and other organizations incorporate robotics and automation technology into their workflow.

INDEX